# FIRST KIDS

## The True Stories of All the Presidents' Children

# FIRST KIDS

## The True Stories of All the Presidents' Children

### ★★★ Noah McCullough ★★★

**■ SCHOLASTIC**

# DEDICATION

To my incredible parents! The "First Kids" had amazing parents. God has blessed me with the very best ever made Mom and Dad. I Love You!

ISBN-13: 978-0-545-17538-8
ISBN-10: 0-545-17538-0

10 9 8 7 6 5 4 3 2 1        09 10 11 12 13

Printed in the U.S.A.   23
First printing, April 2009

Book design by Kay Petronio
Cover design by Becky Terhune

# ★CONTENTS

When I think back on my time at the White House, I recall being just seventeen and suddenly thrust into the limelight as the youngest member of the family and only daughter of the new president chosen by history to replace Richard Nixon.

Susan Ford takes photos of President Ford inside the Oval Office.

Reviewing the many stories in this book brings back fond memories of my own: being the only one of the Ford children to live full-time with my parents in the White House; having my senior prom at the White House, which was very cool; being featured on the cover of Seventeen magazine; discovering a love for photography by following around my dad's team of photographers; being my father's "date" at the Diplomatic reception when my mom was diagnosed with breast cancer; surprising my father with a gift of Liberty, our wonderful golden retriever; and, when I was just eighteen, traveling to China with both of my parents, and meeting Communist Party Chairman Mao Tse-tung.

These were incredibly broadening and formative experiences, and I treasure these memories that shaped and which have continued to influence my life.

Susan Ford Bales

George Washington with his wife, Martha, and two stepchildren.

# The Washingtons

## George Washington (1789-1797)

President Washington sculpted our government as we know it today. He helped win the American Revolution and would be known as America's only six-star general. Washington become the image we see each and every day on the one-dollar bill in our wallets. The funny thing is, the Father of Our Country had no kids of his own.

He married Martha Dandridge Custis, who was a widow with two children. Some historians believe that George married Martha because she owned the largest estate in Virginia and because her late husband left her 30,000 pounds of Virginia currency (equivalent to several million dollars by today's standards). Whether for love or the love of money, they would enjoy a nearly forty-one-year marriage.

## JOHN "JACKY" PARKE CUSTIS

was a young child when George Washington married his mom. He was born in 1754. Jacky only lived to be twenty-seven. He did join the army and served briefly as Washington's aide in the Revolutionary War. His duties were short-lived, however;

he died of fever soon after joining the army and war efforts. He left behind a wife and four small children. George and Martha raised Jacky's two youngest children: Eleanor Parke Custis, also known as Nelly, and her brother George Washington Parke Custis, often called Little Wash. Nelly at age ten and Little Wash at age eight became the first kids to live in a president's house. The first family lived in New York and then in Philadelphia.

## MARTHA "PATSY" PARKE CUSTIS

was born to Martha Washington and her first husband, Daniel Parke Custis, in 1756. George Washington loved Patsy as his own daughter. Unfortunately, Patsy died of epilepsy on June 19, 1773, at the age of seventeen.

The Washingtons with General Lafayette at Mount Vernon in Virginia.

Jacky and Patsy Custis.

# FAST FACTS

★ Geaorge and Martha Washington never lived in the White House but both of their portraits hang there today.

★ Martha Washington was the first American woman to appear on currency—the one-dollar silver certificate in 1886.

★ Mrs. Washington required Nelly to take three piano lessons per week.

★ Nelly spent her adult life taking care of her grandparents, George and Martha Washington.

★ Nelly had a total of eight kids. Four of them would die before they turned two years of age.

★ Little Wash attended St. John's College and Princeton University.

★ Little Wash became a commissioned officer in the military.

★ President Washington never officially adopted Little Wash.

★ Little Wash had four kids. Mary Custis was the only one to survive childhood.

★ Mary married Robert E. Lee, who would become the general in charge of the Confederate army.

★ Little Wash was the author of *Recollection and Private Memoirs of Washington*. He died before it was printed.

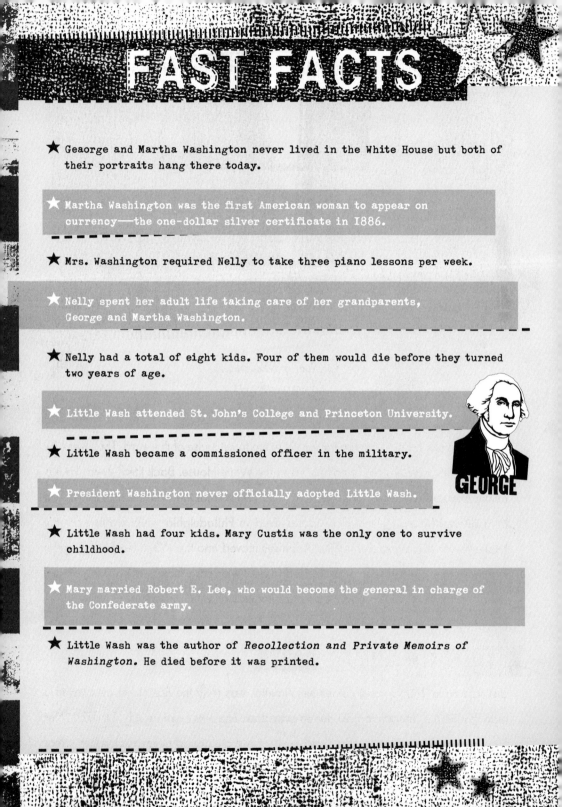

GEORGE

# The John Adamses

## John Adams
## (1797-1801)

The Adams family was the first family in the truest sense of the word. They were the very first presidential family to live in the White House. Back then, it was known as the Executive Mansion. Most people don't realize that the White House was being built during this time. President Adams lived in Philadelphia while waiting for the White House to be completed. The Adamses moved into the White House during the last four months of his term and still had to deal with construction rubble and a yard full of weeds. The very first, first kids were not kids at all; they were grown-ups by the time their dad was elected president.

## ABIGAIL ADAMS SMITH,

also known as Nabby and sometimes Amelia, was truly the first kid to be born to a man that would become an American president. She was born on July 14, 1765. Her life was not a happy one. She lived most of her childhood never seeing her father because he was working in different countries for long periods of time. When she was seventeen, she fell in love, but her dad did not like her boyfriend. President Adams did not believe he was good enough for his daughter and tried to keep them apart. Eventually, her father changed his mind, but by then Nabby had lost contact with her boyfriend and married William Stephens Smith. Nabby died from breast cancer at the age of forty-eight on August 15, 1813.

# JOHN QUINCY ADAMS

was the first son born to a man who would become a U.S. president. He was born on July 11, 1767. He would also become the first son of a president to become president—our sixth. J.Q. was the sharpest child in the family. When he was eleven years old, he lived with his dad in France. John Adams was amazed when his son mastered the French language months before he did. John Quincy lived until age eighty and had an impressive résumé that included Harvard graduate, lawyer, senator, and professor. He was appointed minister to Russia and later negotiated a treaty that would help end the War of 1812 with England. John Quincy Adams was part of President James Monroe's cabinet, serving as secretary of state. Though he would never receive public credit for it, he wrote the Monroe Doctrine, which forbade other countries from staking any claims on U.S. soil.

John Quincy Adams became president because the House of Representatives determined the final election results. Neither candidate had enough electoral

John Quincy Adams at age sixteen.

votes to win, so the House chose John Quincy Adams over Andrew Jackson. It seems John Quincy had offered one of the congressmen a place in his new cabinet. Scandal and corruption followed J.Q. for four painful, nonproductive years until he was defeated miserably for reelection. He died on February 23, 1848.

## SUSANNA ADAMS

lived only a little more than a year. She was born on December 28, 1768, and died on February 4, 1770. It was very common for babies at that time to die in infancy.

## CHARLES ADAMS

was a middle child. He was born on May 29, 1770. Charles had a unique childhood, starting with his move to Europe with his older brother and his dad. As the trip grew tougher, Charles's dad sent him back to his mother and sister, Nabby, in America. Abigail insisted on a chaperone for Charles's trip home. He was eleven years old when his ship set sail from England for the return home. There were problems with this ship, and it was sent to a Spanish port for repairs. No one heard from Charles again for months. He was missing and was considered dead or lost at sea. After five months of family anguish, Charles eventually found his way home.

Charles went to Harvard and had two kids with his wife, Sarah. Then his life began to spiral downward. He abandoned his family at one point and lost a large sum of his brother's money with bad investments. He became addicted to alcohol and fell into a depression. He died at the age of thirty on November 30, 1800. His daughter Susanna lived in the White House with her grandparents and was the first little kid to live there. Susanna was difficult, cranky, and had a hot temper. In fact, one time a friend came over to play and accidentally broke some of the dishes in Susanna's tea set. Susan retaliated by taking the head off of her friend's doll.

13

# THOMAS BOYLSTON ADAMS

was born on September 15, 1772. He went to many of the same schools as his older brother Charles. He followed in his brother's footsteps, graduating from Harvard in 1790. Thomas moved to Philadelphia so he could practice law. He married his sweetheart, Ann Harod. Thomas was appointed as his dad's personal secretary while John Adams was president. He was a judge in the Massachusetts state court system and a successful author, but he didn't seem cut out for a life as a lawyer or politician. The pressure caused him to become dependent on alcohol. He and his wife had seven children. After his death at age fifty-nine on March 13, 1832, all the children moved in with their grandparents and only one married, but had no children.

*"My children give me more pain than all my enemies."*
— John Adams

# FAST FACTS

★ John Adams loved to play with his grandkids in the White House. He often used the White House kitchen as a playground.

★ President Adams had special stables built at the White House for his horse, Cleopatra.

**JOHN ADAMS**

★ President John Adams and his son, John Quincy Adams, were two presidents born on the same street in the same city—Franklin Street in Quincy (formerly Braintree), Massachusetts.

★ Abigail Adams used the empty East Room as a laundry room.

★ Nabby was disfigured from smallpox.

★ John Quincy was a very good billiards player.

★ John Quincy read through the Bible each year.

★ As a little boy, John Quincy witnessed the Battle of Bunker Hill.

★ Charles graduated from Harvard at age nineteen.

★ When Charles abandoned his wife and children, his father said that Charles "had become a madman possessed by the devil."

★ Thomas actually lived in the White House with his parents when he was twenty-eight.

★ History records that Thomas most likely shared a bedroom at the White House with his cousin, Billy Shaw; it is believed to be the room known today as the Green Room.

*"The happiest moments of my life have been the few which I have passed at home in the bosom of my family."*
— Thomas Jefferson

# The Jeffersons

## Thomas Jefferson (1801-1809)

Thomas Jefferson wrote the Declaration of Independence and invented the swivel chair and letter copier. He was a statesman, a musician, and a devoted husband and father. Four of his six children died in infancy or early childhood. After the first three died, his wife, Martha, became depressed and frail. She died when their sixth and last child was only four months old. Mysteriously, when Jefferson died, it was clear that he did not consider his presidency as one of his greatest triumphs. He designed his own tombstone, which reads: "Here was buried Thomas Jefferson, author of the Declaration of American Independence, of the statute of Virginia for religious freedom, and father of the University of Virginia."

## MARTHA "PATSY" WASHINGTON JEFFERSON RANDOLPH

was born to Thomas and Martha Jefferson on September 27, 1772. Martha was one of two Jefferson children who lived to be an adult. She was almost ten when her mom died. Her dad was devastated by the death of his wife. Martha, now known as Patsy, tried everything to make her father happy, almost taking her mother's place. Patsy and her dad became very close. Through all the deaths and depression, Thomas Jefferson accepted an appointment to help negotiate peace with England and make treaties with France. He took Patsy with him.

Thomas Jefferson's daughter, Patsy.

Patsy would outlive her entire family. She married and gave birth to twelve kids. Only one died in early childhood. Her husband, Thomas Randolph, was mentally unstable and bad with the couple's finances. Patsy's kids were the delight of Thomas Jefferson during his presidency. Patsy died on October 10, 1836. She was sixty-four.

## JANE RANDOLPH JEFFERSON

would not live to her second birthday. She was born on April 3, 1774, and died in September 1775.

## BABY BOY JEFFERSON

lived only seventeen short days. He was born on May 28, 1777, and died on June 14, 1777.

## MARY "POLLY" JEFFERSON EPPES

was born on August 1, 1788. At a young age, Polly was left for six years with an aunt while her sister, Martha, and her dad traveled to France. Even though her dad

wanted her to join him and Martha, Polly refused because she felt her home was with her aunt and cousins. One day while playing hide-and-seek on an anchored ship, Polly fell asleep. When she woke up, she realized the ship was moving and they were on the way to France. Polly didn't know this was all planned by her dad. She would barely recognize her dad and sister because they had been away so long. Thomas Jefferson eventually decided to return his family to America. Polly married her cousin Jack Eppes, and he became a successful congressman for the state of Virginia. Polly died just eight weeks after giving birth to her third child, on April 17, 1804. Thomas Jefferson was in his second term in the White House. Polly was only twenty-five years old.

## LUCY ELIZABETH JEFFERSON

lived barely half a year. Born on November 3, 1780, she was named for her dad's sisters. She died on April 15, 1781, and the cause of death is unknown.

## LUCY ELIZABETH JEFFERSON II

was named for her late older sister. She was born on May 8, 1782. She died of whooping cough on October 13, 1784, while living with her aunt and sister Polly. Thomas Jefferson received the bad news while he was in Paris.

# FAST FACTS

★ Thomas Jefferson's oldest daughter, Patsy, occasionally served as his hostess as well as Dolley Madison while Jefferson was president.

★ Patsy allowed her father to choose the names of all of her children.

★ Patsy was said to resemble her father because of her height and red hair.

★ Thomas Jefferson was troubled by Patsy's request to become a nun when she was attending Abbaye de Panthémont (a Catholic school). The Jeffersons were Protestants, and he promptly removed her from the school.

★ Patsy inherited the debts of her husband and father. She sold the family estate at Monticello and its contents to pay the bills.

★ Patsy's second son, James Madison Randolph, was born in the White House and named after James Madison, who was a close friend of Thomas Jefferson.

★ Patsy would often load her kids in her carriage at Monticello and travel to the White House. This trip took three days.

★ Eventually, Patsy and her kids would live in the White House with her dad.

★ Thomas Jefferson kept a lock of hair from his daughter Lucy Elizabeth I in a drawer beside his bed.

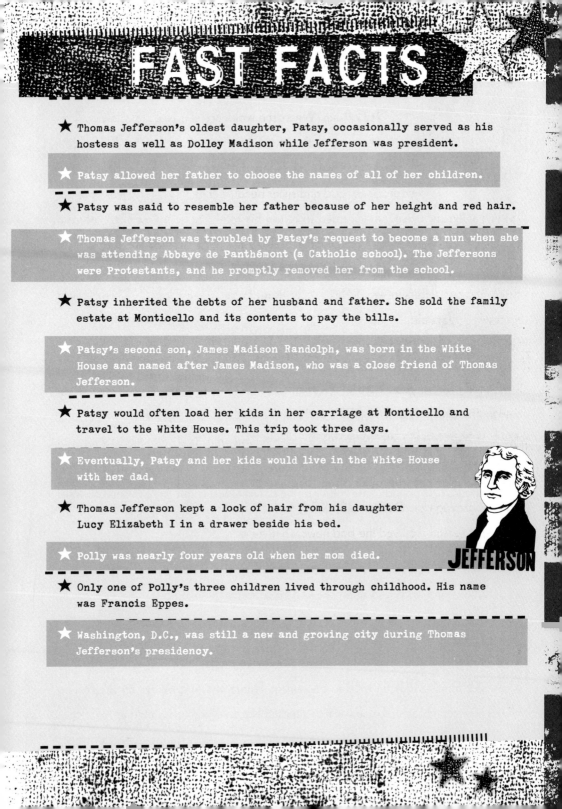

JEFFERSON

★ Polly was nearly four years old when her mom died.

★ Only one of Polly's three children lived through childhood. His name was Francis Eppes.

★ Washington, D.C., was still a new and growing city during Thomas Jefferson's presidency.

President Madison and his wife, Dolley.

# The Madisons

*James Madison (1809-1817)*

J ames and Dolley Madison had no children of their own. Dolley had one living son from a previous marriage named John Payne Todd, who was known as Payne. Her second son, William, died at the age of three months in 1793. Payne lived with the Madisons in the White House when James Madison was president. At 5 feet 6 inches and 100 pounds, this Father of the Constitution is our smallest and shortest president to date. But power sometimes comes in small packages. President Madison not only helped author the Constitution, but also fought hard to add the Bill of Rights and won! His wife, Dolley, is among the most colorful first ladies in our history. She wore turbans and boas and often chewed tobacco and smoked.

## JOHN PAYNE TODD

was adopted by James Madison when he married Dolley in 1794. Payne was two years old. James Madison tried to encourage Payne in several ways by appointing him as his personal secretary as well as sending him on diplomatic missions to Europe. Payne's mind, however, would not be on diplomacy, but instead on gambling, drinking, and dating women. The only thing his parents received from Payne during his travels was his mounting debts. This eventually led Dolley to sell the family plantation at Montpelier to cover what Payne owed. Payne ended up in prison again and again for his gambling and would become an alcoholic. He died in 1852.

# FAST FACTS

★ James Madison was the smallest U.S. President. He weighed only 100 pounds and was 5' 6" tall.

★ During the Madisons' stay at the White House, the British attempted to burn it down. Payne's mom, Dolley Madison, saved several famous things, including the official portrait of George Washington that still hangs in the White House today.

★ The Madisons would not get to live in the White House again due to the fire.

★ The government hired the original architect, James Hoban, to rebuild the White House back to its previous form and stature.

★ This rebuilding would take well into the next administration to complete.

**JAMES MADISON**

★ The first Easter Egg Roll was held by Dolley Madison on the grounds of the Capitol.

★ Dolley Madison introduced ice cream to the White House.

★ Payne admitted on his deathbed at age sixty-one that he had only harmed himself. What he failed to realize is that he also harmed his mom and dad financially.

# The Monroes

*James Monroe (1817-1825)*

The Monroes didn't get to live in the White House right away. It was still under reconstruction. Monroe was a popular president and when he ran for reelection, he ran unopposed. James Monroe preferred speaking French to English and was the first president to fulfill the office of secretary of state and secretary of war at the same time. Monroe is one of three U.S. presidents to have died on the most patriotic day of the year, the Fourth of July. The other two presidents who died on July 4 were John Adams and Thomas Jefferson. The Monroes had two daughters and a son.

## ELIZA KORTRIGHT MONROE HAY

was the first daughter of James and Elizabeth Monroe. She was born on December 5, 1786. She married attorney George Hay. She served as hostess for her mother, who refused to socialize with heads of state. Eliza had a definite style of entertaining, different from the "normal" social scene in Washington. During her eight-year reign as hostess, filling in for her mom, Eliza managed to offend and alienate many politicians' wives. She rarely held any social events, and when she did, she invited very few of

Washington's elite social group. When Elizabeth hosted her sister Maria's wedding, she sent out almost no invitations to friends, family, dignitaries, foreign leaders, or important politicians. The event was not publicized properly, and there were very few people in attendance, no gifts, and nothing much to remember. Maria never forgot or forgave her older sister's lack of effort and eventually the two stopped speaking. Eliza died in 1835 at the age of forty-nine.

## JAMES SPENCE MONROE

was the first and only son of James and Elizabeth Monroe. Unfortunately, he didn't survive childhood. He was born in May 1799 and died on September 28, 1801.

## MARIA HESTER MONROE GOUVERNEUR

was the youngest daughter of the Monroes. She was born in 1803. Maria lived in France until the age of four. She was a young teenager when her dad became president and she definitely enjoyed the spotlight that came with it. She was active and had a vibrant personality. She fell in love with one of her dad's staff members and became the first child of a president to be married in the White House. The couple moved to New York City, where her husband, Samuel Gouverneur, was appointed postmaster. She and her husband were financially secure and eventually had three children. Maria lived to be forty-seven years old, dying in 1850.

# FAST FACTS

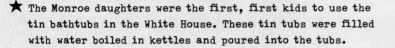

★ The Monroe daughters were the first, first kids to use the tin bathtubs in the White House. These tin tubs were filled with water boiled in kettles and poured into the tubs.

★ During Monroe's administration, a curved iron fence replaced the stone wall around the White House.

**JAMES MONROE**

★ Eliza was often her father's spokesperson when he was president.

★ Eliza's daughter lived in the White House during her grandfather's administration. Her name was Hortensia Hay, after the queen of Holland.

★ Eliza's son, James, was unable to speak or hear.

★ Eliza's husband, George Hay, was most known for being the prosecuting attorney in the famous treason trial of Aaron Burr (Thomas Jefferson's vice president).

★ Maria had a life of firsts. Not only was she the first, first kid to marry in the White House, but she married her first cousin, Samuel Gouveneur.

★ Maria started the fashion craze of wearing pants. They were called pantalettes.

★ Some of the elegant furniture purchased by the Monroes remains in the White House today.

★ The Monroes ordered the first presidential china. The pattern had a large eagle in the middle that is known as the Monroe eagle. First Lady Lady Bird Johnson used the Monroe eagle on the Johnson presidential china.

President Adams and his wife, Louisa.

# The John Quincy Adamses

## John Quincy Adams (1825-1829)

John Quincy Adams was an extremely driven first kid. He achieved things that some of us can only dream of. He was a foreign minister, secretary of state, the president, and was even a congressman after his presidency. Some would argue that it was his father, John Adams, who was doing the driving. John Quincy would be no different with his own children. Though he raised one extremely successful child, he would ultimately drive two of his three sons to early deaths with his extreme standards and high expectations. John Adams, John Quincy's father, regretted his parenting style with his own children, and as a grandfather decided to be a friend. Things weren't much better for Mrs. John Quincy Adams. Louisa had virtually no friends in Washington.

## GEORGE WASHINGTON ADAMS

was born on April 12, 1801. John Quincy Adams hoped his son would become a prominent lawyer and enter into the political arena. However, George had plans of his own and was interested in literature, poetry, drama, and music. This did not please his presidential father. He unfortunately was in love with his cousin until she started dating his brother, whom she ultimately married. This devastated and embarrassed George. He never recovered  and fell into depression. Eventually, he became an alcoholic, and was debt-ridden. He mismanaged his parents' business affairs and was going to meet with his father when he began hallucinating. While on a ship bound for Washington, George committed suicide on April 30, 1829, at the age of twenty-eight by jumping overboard and drowning.

## JOHN ADAMS II

was born on July 4, 1803. He was wild and athletic. He was once expelled from Harvard for taking part in a student riot. John II was the Adams son who ended up marrying his cousin, which caused a huge rift among his brothers. None of the family attended his wedding in protest. He did everything he could to never follow his father's advice and did not seem to care if he displeased him. He, too, became an alcoholic and died in the prime of his life at the age of thirty-one, on October 23, 1834.

## CHARLES FRANCIS ADAMS

came along on August 18, 1807. By age seven, he had traveled to three different countries. He is the only Adams son who seemed to respond positively to the pressure  of his father. He graduated from Harvard Law School and represented Massachusetts in the House of Representatives. The Adams legacy of his dad and grandfather would continue, with Charles becoming an ambassador to Great Britain. Charles single-handedly convinced the British not to aid the Confederacy in the Civil War. The Union victory was partially due to his negotiations. His name was considered for president in several elections, but his ideas were not popular enough. He spoke French, German, and Russian fluently. He outlived both of his brothers and died at age seventy-nine on November 21, 1886.

# LOUISA CATHERINE ADAMS

was the only daughter born to John Quincy and Louisa Adams. She was born in 1811 and died in 1812 while her family was living in Russia.

> "No one knows the agonies I suffer."
> — John Quincy Adams, about his son George

# FAST FACTS

★ All three Adams kids attended Harvard.

★ George won a poetry contest that included a competitor named Ralph Waldo Emerson.

**JOHN QUINCY**

★ George never married.

★ George was a member of the Massachusetts State Legislature.

★ George was a captain in the militia.

★ John II was his father's secretary during the 1825—1829 term.

★ John II was challenged to a duel by one of his father's critics.

★ John II managed the family-operated business, and it failed.

★ John II's father, John Quincy, was at his side when he died.

★ Charles Francis ran for vice president on the Free Soil ticket.

★ Charles Francis authored political pamphlets and wrote for political magazines.

★ Charles Francis actually edited his grandparents' letters (John and Abigail Adams).

★ Charles Francis was offered the opportunity to be the president of Harvard in 1869. He turned down the job.

# The Jacksons

*Andrew Jackson*
*(1829-1837)*

Andrew Jackson, also known as Old Hickory, was an established war hero, a lawyer, governor, congressman, president, and a proud adoptive father of one child. Jackson was married for thirty-seven years, but he and his wife, Rachel, had no biological kids. This tough-as-nails president seemed to have a soft side as well. Many times the Jacksons played parents to several nephews, as well as some orphans. All in all the Jacksons were said to have raised and help educate eleven children.

## ANDREW JACKSON JR.

was born on December 4, 1808. This baby was actually President Jackson's nephew. The baby was one of the twins born to Rachel Jackson's brother. The babies' mom was convinced that she could not care for both, so one was sent to the Jacksons to raise. They adopted him, naming him Andrew Jackson Jr., or Andy. Andy, though loved by his father, was a disappointment. He seemed to hang out with the wrong crowd. He was engaged two times before his marriage to Sarah Yorke. They had one daughter

and one son together. Andy was a failure at managing money and accumulated debt after debt that President Jackson paid off.

When Jackson Sr. willed his own estate, the Hermitage, and all of his financial holdings to Andy Jr., he failed again. This time the failure required selling the Hermitage and the surrounding land to the state of Tennessee. The state did allow him to live there for the remainder of his life. He died twenty years after his father in 1865 from lockjaw.

Andrew Jackson Jr.

# FAST FACTS

★ Lots of family on Jackson's side as well as his wife's side lived in the White House during his presidency.

★ President Jackson loved the idea of becoming a grandfather. He gave Andy Jr. and Sarah some of his wife Rachel's jewelry with the stipulation that it would be given to their daughter if they were to have one.

★ President Jackson urged his son and daughter-in-law to come and live in the White House, probably to keep Andy Jr. from running up more bills.

★ President Jackson would allow his rambunctious granddaughter, Rachel, to interrupt Cabinet meetings whenever she wanted.

★ Andy Jr.'s debt totaled more than $4,800. This was a large amount at the time considering the average yearly salary for a Tennessee family was around $300.

★ Two women served in the role of first lady during Andrew Jackson's presidency due to the fact that his wife had died. Emily Donelson, his wife's niece, and Sarah Yorke Jackson, his daugher-in-law.

★ Andy Jr. had an alcohol problem most of his adult life.

★ Andy Jr. accidentally shot himself in the hand. This led to the lockjaw that killed him.

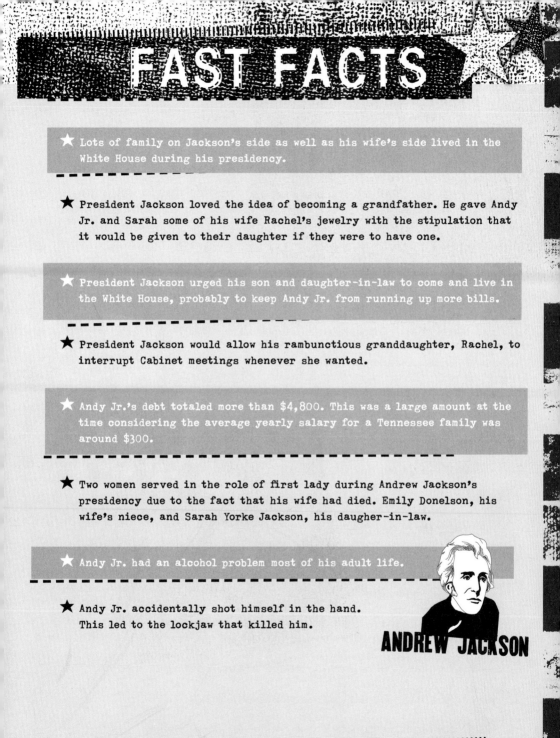

ANDREW JACKSON

# First Families Play Games

**BILLIARDS:** John Quincy Adam's boys, Abe Lincoln, the Grants, the Garfields, the Benjamin Harrisons, Woodrow Wilson, the Carters

**BOGGLE:** the Clintons

**BRIDGE:** the Tafts, Edith Wilson, the Hardings, Bess Truman, Dwight Eisenhower, Mamie Eisenhower, Lady Bird Johnson, Luci Johnson Nugent, Lynda Johnson Robb

**CHECKERS:** Andrew Johnson, Calvin Coolidge Jr.

**CHARADES:** Alice Roosevelt Longworth, the Taft kids, the Kennedys

**CHESS:** Abe Lincoln, James Madison, James Garfield, Rutherford B. Hayes, the Hardings, Rosalynn Carter, Amy Carter

**CRIBBAGE:** Grover Cleveland, the McKinleys

**DOMINOES:** the Hardings, Lyndon Johnson

**EUCHRE:** the Tafts, Grover Cleveland, the McKinleys

**GIN RUMMY:** Anna Roosevelt

**HIDE–AND–SEEK:** Scott and Fanny Hayes, Quentin and Archie Roosevelt, the Taft kids

**JIGSAW PUZZLES:** Calvin Coolidge

**LOO:** Dolley Madison, Elizabeth Monroe, Eliza Monroe Hay

**MAH–JONGG:** Florence Harding

**POKER:** Warren Harding, Franklin Delano Roosevelt, Harry Truman, Dwight Eisenhower, Richard Nixon

**SOLITAIRE:** Woodrow Wilson, Franklin Delano Roosevelt, Mamie Eisenhower

**TWENTY QUESTIONS:** the Taft kids, Eleanor Roosevelt

**WHIST:** Dolley Madison, the John Quincy Adamses, James Garfield

President Van Buren and his wife, Hannah.

# The Van Burens

*Martin Van Buren*
*(1837-1841)*

P resident Martin Van Buren was known as the little magician. His political magic seemed to also work on his children. His kids were pretty successful. One was even a presidential candidate! His four sons were close friends throughout his entire life. He was married to his cousin, Hannah Hoes, and she died at the age of thirty-five (eighteen years before her husband was elected president), two years after she had given birth to a fifth son.

## ABRAHAM VAN BUREN

was born on November 27, 1807. Abraham was devoted to his father. He was only sixteen when he left for college at West Point. He would be the first of the Van Buren boys to be a college graduate. The famous Dolley Madison introduced her niece Angelica Singleton to Abraham. A year later, they were married. Angelica was considered elegant and refined. She acted as President Van Buren's first lady. Abraham joined the military and rose to the rank of lieutenant colonel. He resigned his position to become his father's secretary in the White House, but he eventually got his wish of being a war hero. History notes that Abraham served with bravery in the Mexican War of 1854. He died on March 15, 1873.

## JOHN VAN BUREN

was the Van Buren boy with the most personality and style. Born on February 10, 1810, he was considered extremely talented, brilliant, and good-looking. As a teenager, he graduated from Yale and passed the New York bar at age twenty. He traveled in Europe for a while and returned home to open his own law practice in New York. He settled down and married Elizabeth Van der Poel. Even with his partying reputation, he became interested in politics and made his way to Washington, D.C. He was elected repeatedly to the U.S. House of Representatives. John had an incurable zest for life. He returned to Europe one last time with his only child and would not make it back to America alive. He died aboard the ship from kidney failure on October 13, 1866.

John Van Buren (circa 1855–1865).

# MARTIN "MAT" VAN BUREN JR.

was born a few years after his famous brother John on December 20, 1812. His entire life seemed to be dedicated to his father. He not only followed him to the White House, but he spent all of his life serving him. He was small in stature and quiet. He was his father's secretary and eventually organized all of the Van Buren presidential papers. Because Mat was so concerned with only serving his father, he had no social life and poor health. He would die on March 19, 1855, at age forty-two.

# LAWRENCE VAN BUREN

was born and died in 1814.

# SMITH THOMPSON VAN BUREN

was born on January 16, 1817, and was named after his dad's best friend from the New York Supreme Court. Though dedicated to his dad, Smith did have a private life. History provides little information about it other than he was married twice and had seven kids. He defended his father's political actions and became his main spokesperson and speechwriter. He really never had a political agenda of his own but was more about his dad's political life and career. He died in 1876 at age fifty-nine.

# FAST FACTS

VAN BUREN

★ The Van Burens were accused of extreme and lavish spending because they spruced up the White House by painting, replacing carpet, installing new chandeliers, etc.

★ The Van Burens actually spent half of what Andrew Jackson did on remodeling when he was in office.

★ The Van Buren boys were the first, first kids to attend their father's inaugural balls when he became president.

★ All the Van Buren boys were grown when their dad was elected president.

★ All the boys lived in the White House at one time or another.

★ Abraham served in the army for eighteen years.

★ Abraham once served as an aide to Zachary Taylor.

★ Abraham and Angelica Van Buren loved to entertain and were known for their lively social gatherings in later years.

★ Abraham helped edit and publish his father's works.

★ John once pulled his father out of bed, covers and all, when he overslept; his dad was vice president at the time.

★ John's flair and his charm earned him the nickname Prince John.

★ John had celebrity status in Washington, D.C.

★ John did not support slavery, but he also did not support Abraham Lincoln in his bid for the presidency.

★ Mat was the first, first son to die in a foreign country (France).

★ Mat never married.

★ Smith was a law student while living in the White House.

★ Smith completed and edited his father's treatise on the development of political parties.

★ Smith served as a secretary to his father.

# The William Henry Harrisons

## William Henry Harrison (1841)

William Henry Harrison and his wife, Anna Tuthill Symmes Harrison, planned for a very large family. They had ten children together. In fact, when Harrison ran for president, he and his vice president, John Tyler, were referred to as the fertility ticket because they had so many children between them (Harrison with ten and Tyler with eight at the time—that's a combined total of eighteen kids)! Unfortunately, only three of the Harrison kids would make it past their thirty-fifth birthday. Mrs. Harrison was very ill when her husband became president. She eventually recovered before the president died. She would bury her husband and nine of her ten children before she died.

## ELIZABETH "BETSEY" BASSETT HARRISON SHORT

was born on September 29, 1796. She did not know her father in childhood because he was always gone. She married her cousin, John Short, and lived on a farm owned by her dad. She was one of four Harrison first kids to be alive when William became president. She died on September 26, 1846.

## JOHN CLEVES SYMMES HARRISON,

the first-born son, made his appearance on October 28, 1798, in Indiana. John was well-respected by local farmers and settlers in the Indiana Territory where he lived. He was known for his honesty and was appointed to a position in the government land office. At the time he was serving in this position, his dad, General Harrison, had many political enemies. John was eventually accused of stealing a large sum of money (around $13,000) from the government. Some historians think that people who hated his father set him up and the evidence was hidden. He died at the young age of thirty-two on October 30, 1830.

## LUCY SINGLETON HARRISON ESTE

was born on September 5, 1800, and was a teenager when she married her husband, David Este, a Superior Court of Ohio judge. She had four kids before she died at age twenty-five on April 7, 1826.

## WILLIAM HENRY HARRISON JR.

was born on September 3, 1802. He would only live thirty-five years because of his alcoholism. He graduated from Transylvania College in Kentucky, married, and had a brief law career before his untimely death on February 6, 1838.

## JOHN SCOTT HARRISON

was born on October 4, 1804. He was the only first kid to be the son of a president and the father of a president. John was the father of Benjamin Harrison, the twenty-third president of the United States. He named his famous son after his brother Benjamin. He was elected to two terms in the House of Representatives and was a popular leader and politician. He was married twice and had nine children. He died at age seventy-three on May 25, 1878, outliving his entire family of first brothers and sisters.

# BENJAMIN HARRISON

was born on May 5, 1806. Benjamin achieved the ultimate goal of his presidential father, when he went to college and became a doctor. He became a physician and opened his own practice. His business was going well until he was abducted and taken prisoner during the Texas War of Independence. The Mexican army needed a doctor, and they "selected" him for the job. Benjamin died a couple of months before his dad was elected president on June 9, 1840. He was thirty-four years old.

# MARY SYMMES HARRISON THORNTON

was born on January 22, 1809. History does not give a lot of details about this first daughter's life other than she married a doctor and had six kids before she died on November 16, 1842.

# CARTER BASSETT HARRISON

was born on October 26, 1811. He would only live to be twenty-seven. He was an attorney and practiced law. He married Mary Anne Sutherland and had one child. He died on August 12, 1839.

# ANNA TUTHILL HARRISON TAYLOR

was named after her mother, Anna Tuthill Symmes. She was born on October 28, 1813. She married her cousin, William Henry Harrison Taylor, who was named after her father. Historians argue over the exact year of her death. Some say 1845 and others say 1865. Some say she had no children. Others say she had six. Nevertheless, she would witness her father's election to the presidency.

# JAMES FINDLAY HARRISON

was the only Harrison first kid to die in childhood. He was born on May 15, 1814. He was named after one of his dad's friends. He died in 1817.

# FAST FACTS

★ President and Mrs. Harrison had a total of 48 grandkids and 106 great-grandchildren.

★ The Harrison family is the only first family to have four generations alive at the time of their inauguration.

★ President Harrison was the first dad of a first kid to die in office.

HARRISON

★ John married Clarissa Pike, the only daughter of Zebulon Pike, who is credited with discovering Pike's Peak in the state of Colorado.

★ After his death, John's dad paid back the government the amount of money John was accused of embezzling.

★ William Jr. served as his father's aide when he was serving as minister to Mexico.

★ William Jr.'s widow served as interim first lady for his father, William Henry Harrison.

★ John was a popular congressman but preferred farming to politics.

★ Benjamin was the only first kid to have a president named after him. His nephew, the son of John Scott Harrison, was the 23rd president, Benjamin Harrison.

★ Mary died one year after her dad was inaugurated.

★ Carter traveled with his dad to South America when General Harrison was appointed minister to Colombia.

★ Carter and his dad returned home to America following a revolution in Colombia.

★ Anna was born weeks after her dad's involvement in the War of 1812.

# First Kids Who Married in the White House

## (While Dad was President)

MARIA MONROE AND SAMUEL GOUVERNEUR

JOHN ADAMS AND MARY CATHERINE HELLEN

LIZZIE TYLER AND WILLIAM WALLER

NELLIE GRANT AND ALGERNON SARTORIS

ALICE ROOSEVELT AND NICHOLAS LONGWORTH

JESSIE WILSON AND FRANCIS SAYRE

NELLIE WILSON AND WILLIAM MCADOO

LUCI BAINES JOHNSON AND PATRICK NUGENT (RECEPTION ONLY)

LYNDA BIRD JOHNSON AND CHARLES ROBB

TRICIA NIXON AND ED COX

# The Tylers

## John Tyler (1841-1845)

ohn Tyler was the 10th president of the United States. He was the first vice president ever to become president by the death of a president. President Tyler suffered much criticism for taking full command of the presidency instead of filling in for the president who had just died. His cabinet wanted to make all the decisions for him. During his presidency, his beloved wife, Letitia, died. President Tyler was heartbroken. Not long after his first wife's death, he married Julia Gardiner, who was thirty years younger than him! This ultimately caused a huge rift in his family. Tyler's popularity didn't get any better. He was considered a traitor by the North for serving in the Confederate Congress from 1861 to 1862. On the homefront, John Tyler was sure to have felt like the president of a small country as the father of fifteen children.

## MARY TYLER JONES

was born on April 15, 1815. She was John Tyler's first child. Mary found her true love in Henry Jones, a farmer. She actually gave birth to one of her two kids inside the

White House. She had been visiting her parents while her mother was ill, and had her second son, a boy named Robert who grew up to fight for the Confederacy. Mary died unexpectedly at age thirty-three on June 17, 1848.

# ROBERT TYLER

was born on September 9, 1816. Robert grew up to be a successful man. He married Elizabeth Priscilla Cooper, who would serve as acting first lady for Robert's dad. At the same time, Robert served as his dad's personal secretary. After the Civil War ended, he moved to Alabama and began a law practice. His practice struggled financially. Robert regained his financial edge by becoming the editor for *The Advisor*, a Montgomery newspaper. He died on December 3, 1877, at the age of sixty-one.

# JOHN TYLER JR.

was born on April 17, 1819. He grew up to become an amazing writer. A newspaper editor once insulted his father so much that John challenged him to a duel. When the newspaper editor didn't show up, John was instantly launched into popularity. John then met Martha Rochelle, whom he married. Together they had three kids. He died on January 26, 1896, at the age of seventy-six.

# LETITIA TYLER SEMPLE

was born on May 11, 1821. Letitia had one goal in life: to be close to her father. She helped her dad with many things, including acting as the first lady when her mom was ill. She got to spend a lot of time with her dad because her husband, James Semple, was never around much. When her dad married Julia Gardiner Tyler, Letitia was furious. She would never accept her stepmother. Though close to her in age, Letitia outlived her stepmom and died on December 28, 1907, at the age of eighty-six.

# ELIZABETH "LIZZIE" TYLER WALLER

A children's ball hosted by President Tyler at the White House.

was born on July 11, 1823. Lizzie was known as a vibrant and colorful person. She fell in love with William Waller when she was just eighteen years old. She married him and had an eight-year marriage that produced five kids. Unfortunately, she died on June 1, 1850, at age twenty-six, due to complications relating to childbirth.

# ANNE CONTESSE TYLER

was born in April 1825. She would never live to see her father become president because she only lived for three months, dying in July 1825.

# ALICE TYLER DENISON

was born on March 23, 1827. Alice was usually in boarding schools while her father worked his way toward the presidency. When he became president, she wanted to be a part of the action. She desperately wanted to live in Washington, D.C. Her stepmom sent for her, and she returned to Washington. After her father's term in office ended, she married Harry Denison. Their marriage produced one child. Alice died on June 8, 1854, when she was just twenty-seven years old.

# TAZEWELL TYLER

was born on December 6, 1830. He was only a teenager when his mother died and he suddenly got a stepmom. Because of his education in medical school, he served in the medical corps for the Confederacy. After the war, he practiced medicine in three different states: Virginia, Maryland, and California. He married Nannie Bridges, and they had two kids. He later died of alcoholism at the age of forty-three on January 8, 1874.

# DAVID GARDINER "GARDIE" TYLER

was born on July 12, 1846. David was the first child born to John Tyler and his second wife. David never saw his dad as president because he was born one year after his parents left the White House. He became a lawyer and was admitted to the Virginia bar in 1870. He later followed in his father's footsteps, by being elected to the U.S. Congress. He was a dedicated family man with a wife and four kids. He died on September 5, 1927. He was eighty-one.

# JOHN ALEXANDER "ALEX" TYLER

was born on April 7, 1848. This first kid ran away from home at age fourteen to enlist in the Confederate army but was turned down because of his age. When he was finally old enough to serve, he joined the navy. After his service in the war, he traveled to Germany to study. When this war hero moved back to the United States, he had a hard time finding a job. His luck improved as he soon found a wife, Sarah, and a job as a surveyor. John died on September 1, 1883. He was thirty-five.

# JULIA TYLER SPENCER

was born on December 25, 1849. Julia eventually went to a convent school in Canada. After her studies, she met a man named William Spencer. They fell in love and married. Unfortunately, William sank the young couple into enormous debt. Julia died on May 8, 1871, at the age of twenty-one while giving birth to her only child. Her husband disappeared and was never heard from again.

# LACHLAN TYLER

was born on December 2, 1851. Lachlan's dream was to be a doctor. He worked hard to achieve his dream by going to medical school and getting good grades. He was eventually offered an appointment with the U.S. Navy as a surgeon. While in the service, he also began his own private medical practice. After a while, his practice became so successful that he quit his job in the navy in order to concentrate on it full-time. Lachlan married Georgia Powell and became a very wealthy man. He died at the height of his career on January 25, 1902, at age fifty.

## LYON GARDINER TYLER

was born on August 24, 1853. Lyon was bright and intelligent. He attended the University of Virginia. After school, he went on to be the founder of his own tiny college. He soon moved up in the ranks and became the president of the College of William and Mary, a position he kept for thirty-one years. While serving as the president of this university, Lyon became an author, public speaker, and historian. He married twice and was the father of six kids. Lyon died on February 12, 1935. He was eighty-one.

## ROBERT FITZWALTER "FITZ" TYLER

was born on March 12, 1856. Fitz was intellectually gifted and started his studies at Georgetown University. He didn't get to complete his education because he ran out of money. After his withdrawal from school, he settled on a more simple life. Fitz moved to the country and became a successful farmer. He married but had no kids. Fitz died on December 30, 1927, at the age of sixty-one.

## PEARL TYLER ELLIS

was born on June 20, 1860. Pearl was the last child of President Tyler. She went to Sacred Heart Convent School in Washington, D.C. She moved to Virginia, where she met and married William Ellis. They had eight kids together. Pearl became a homemaker and died on June 30, 1947, at the age of eighty-seven.

# FAST FACTS

★ John Tyler began his White House career as vice president. When William Henry Harrison died unexpectedly, Tyler became president. He was called His Accidency because of his accidental presidency.

★ Letitia Tyler suffered a stroke that paralyzed her. She lived with her family in the White House but could not perform her duties as first lady.

★ Mrs. Tyler was the first wife of a president to die in the White House.

★ Julia Gardiner Tyler, President Tyler's second wife, introduced the new tradition of having "Hail to the Chief" played when the president made an entrance or appearance.

★ Robert eventually became the Alabama Democratic state chairman.

★ Priscilla actually had a secret weapon that helped her get rave reviews as a White House hostess. She was a friend of Dolley Madison, who helped her make things extra elegant and spectacular.

★ John's struggle with alcohol made him unable to fulfill his duties as a husband and father.

★ Letitia owned and operated a private school in Baltimore.

★ Alice married an Episcopalian rector.

TYLER

★ Tazewell studied medicine with his uncle, who was a doctor.

★ David was sixteen when he joined the Confederate army.

★ John Alexander became fluent in German.

★ Julia was born on Christmas Day.

★ When Julia wrote to her dad and told him that the Nova Scotia school was making her seriously consider becoming a nun, he made her come home.

★ Lyon helped the College of William and Mary reopen its doors after it had been forced to close due to lack of funds.

★ As a successful farmer, Fitz's land was near the Tyler home in Sherwood Forest.

★ Pearl's name was originally Margaret, but she was christened Pearl.

# First Kids Working for

| NAME | DAD | POSITION |
|---|---|---|
| Martha Randolph | Thomas Jefferson | Hostess |
| Samuel Gouverneur (son-in-law) | James Monroe | Private secretary |
| George Hay (son-in-law) | James Monroe | Secretary, adviser |
| Eliza Hay | James Monroe | Aide to her mom |
| Charles Adams | John Quincy Adams | Private secretary |
| John Adams II | John Quincy Adams | Private secretary |
| Smith Van Buren | Martin Van Buren | Private secretary |
| Martin Van Buren Jr. | Martin Van Buren | Private secretary |
| Abraham Van Buren | Martin Van Buren | Military aide |
| Angelica Van Buren (daughter-in-law) | Martin Van Buren | Hostess |
| Jane Harrison (daughter-in-law) | William Henry Harrison | Hostess |
| John Tyler Jr. | John Tyler | Private secretary |
| Robert Tyler | John Tyler | Private secretary |
| Priscilla Tyler (daughter-in-law) | John Tyler | Hostess |
| Lizzie Tyler | John Tyler | Assistant hostess |
| Letitia Semple | John Tyler | Hostess |
| William Bliss (son-in-law) | Zachary Taylor | Private secretary |
| Betty Bliss | Zachary Taylor | Hostess |
| Robert Wood (son-in-law) | Zachary Taylor | Doctor to president |

# Dad in the White House

| NAME | DAD | POSITION |
| --- | --- | --- |
| Powers Fillmore | Millard Fillmore | Private secretary |
| Abby Fillmore | Millard Fillmore | Assistant hostess |
| Robert Johnson | Andrew Johnson | Private secretary |
| Martha Patterson | Andrew Johnson | Hostess |
| Mary Stover | Andrew Johnson | Hostess |
| Buck Grant | Ulysses S. Grant | Aide |
| Webb Hayes | Rutherford B. Hayes | Aide |
| Mary McKee | Benjamin Harrison | Assistant hostess |
| Robert McKee (son-in-law) | Benjamin Harrison | Aide |
| Helen Taft | William Howard Taft | Social aide to mom |
| James Roosevelt | Franklin D. Roosevelt | Aide |
| Anna Dall Boettiger | Franklin D. Roosevelt | Aide |
| John Eisenhower | Dwight D. Eisenhower | Aide |
| Barbara Eisenhower (daughter-in-law) | Dwight D. Eisenhower | State trip representative |
| Julie Nixon Eisenhower | Richard M. Nixon | Aide to mom |
| Susan Ford | Gerald R. Ford | Substitute hostess |
| Jack Ford | Gerald R. Ford | Campaign aide |
| Chip Carter | Jimmy Carter | Aide |

# The Polks

## James K. Polk (1845-1849)

ames Polk, the 11th president of the United States, and his wife, Sarah, had no children. Some say this was due to the fact that they had no time because they were working way too hard. Sarah served as President Polk's private secretary while in the White House and it was said they both worked up to sixteen-hour days with very little sleep. They forbade dancing and drinking in the White House and never took a single vacation while they lived and worked there. Though they worked from daylight until dusk, they did allow a few comforts while in the White House. The Polks were the first to have an icebox and gas lights in the Executive Mansion. James Polk served only one term in office by choice . . . he was probably tired. He died only three months after his presidency.

President Taylor (circa 1849) and his wife, Margaret.

# The Taylors

*Zachary Taylor (1849-1850)*

Zachary Taylor was considered the most popular man in America at one time. How could anyone not like this farmer turned war hero? He became the 12th president of the United States of America. Then he died suddenly, a year into the job. Two of the Taylors' six children died as toddlers. Mrs. Taylor often traveled with her military husband. She was determined to give her four remaining children the best education that money could buy, so she packed the kids up and sent them east for schooling.

## ANNE MARGARET MACKALL TAYLOR WOOD

was born in Kentucky on April 9, 1811. As a kid, she moved around a lot to different military posts because of her dad's job. On one of these moves, she met her future husband, Robert Crooke Wood, who was an army surgeon. They married and had four children. Two of her four children served in the Confederate forces while their dad remained dedicated to the Union. After the death of her husband, she moved to

Germany with her daughter, who was married to a German embassy staff member. She lived to be sixty-four years old. She died on December 2, 1875.

# SARAH KNOX TAYLOR DAVIS

was born at Fort Knox on March 6, 1814. Her claim to fame was marrying the future president of the Confederacy, Lieutenant Jefferson Davis. Her parents did not approve of the marriage because Davis had served with Sarah's dad in the Black Hawk War. They disliked each other, and often disagreed. Three months after their marriage, the newlyweds contracted malaria. Davis recovered, but Sarah died on September 15, 1835. She was only twenty-one.

# OCTAVIA PANNEL TAYLOR

was born on August 16, 1816. She died at age three on July 8, 1820, from malaria, which was common at the time.

# MARGARET SMITH TAYLOR

was born on July 27, 1819, in Kentucky. She died at the age of fifteen months on October 22, 1820.

# MARY ELIZABETH "BETTY" TAYLOR BLISS DANDRIDGE

had such a long name, they called her Betty. She was born on April 20, 1824. She married one of her father's military staff. William Wallace Smith Bliss, her groom, was from West Point. He and Betty moved into the White House. William served as a manager of Taylor's business and was in charge of the Executive Mansion, while his wife served as hostess for President Taylor. When her husband died, she married Philip Pendleton Dandridge from Virginia. She lived to be eighty-five years old. She died on July 25, 1909.

# RICHARD "DICK" TAYLOR

was the only son born to Zachary Taylor and his wife, Margaret. He was born on January 27, 1826. As a youth, he attended boarding schools overseas. He didn't see his father for eleven years while in school. When he returned to the United States, he attended Harvard but ended up graduating from Yale. After his dad was elected president, he became Zachary's personal secretary. Prior to this, he had worked the family plantation for a while. After his dad's death, Dick served as a general in the Confederate Army. He eventually married and had five kids of his own. Dick was an active Louisiana politician. He was in poor health when he died on April 12, 1879, at age fifty-three.

*"My wife was as much a soldier as I was."*
— Zachary Taylor

# FAST FACTS

★ President Taylor was a victim of the hot sun during the 1850 4th of July celebrations. He listened to countless speeches and retired to the White House eager for some cool refreshment. Soon he had fever and stomach cramps. He died with the public believing he was poisoned with arsenic.

★ Zachary Taylor was the second president to die in office. Abraham Lincoln gave the eulogy at his funeral.

★ The Taylor family had a favorite White House pet. Old Whitey had been their father's horse from his time in the military. They let him roam free on the lawn of the White House to graze and enjoy life.

★ Visitors to the White House would pluck hairs from Old Whitey's tail as souvenirs.

★ Mrs. Taylor spent most of her time in the White House in her room, knitting and smoking her corncob pipe.

**TAYLOR**

★ Anne's doctor husband became a consulting physician to the president.

★ Anne and her four children frequently visited the White House.

★ Betty was the fun-loving hostess for her father at the White House.

★ Betty had no children.

★ Dick was a state senator for Louisiana when the Civil War began.

★ Dick rose to the rank of general during the Civil War.

★ Dick's book, *Destruction and Reconstruction*, was published exactly one week before he died.

# The Fillmores

*Millard Fillmore*
*(1850-1853)*

illard and Abigail Fillmore were lifelong readers. Millard met Abigail when she was his teacher. Millard became one of the brightest people of the day, serving as a soldier, lawyer, congressman, vice president, and even the president of the United States. Their passion for learning drew them together and they were a team throughout their entire marriage. Millard Fillmore assumed the presidency after Zachary Taylor's sudden death. He raised two bright and charming children and brought them with him into the White House.

## MILLARD POWERS FILLMORE

was born on April 25, 1828. This first kid went by his middle name, Powers. He studied law at Cambridge and moved into the White House with his parents at the age of twenty-four when his dad assumed office. He served as his father's private secretary. Powers never married or had any children. He was a federal court clerk for a time. He was hurt when his father remarried after his mom's death. After his father's death, Powers lived in the Tifft House, a Buffalo, New York, hotel. He became furious when his father left most of his belongings to the second wife. He successfully sued his stepmother, acquiring his father's presidential papers and much of the family inheritance. He died on November 15, 1889, at age sixty-one.

## MARY ABIGAIL "ABBY" FILLMORE

was born March 27, 1832. She was nineteen years old when she moved into the White House. Abby was a wonderful musician and played harp, piano, and guitar. She served as White House hostess during her father's administration, assisting her sickly and weak mom. Abby was so close to her ailing mother that she was heartbroken when she passed away. A year later, Abby died at age twenty-two in 1854. She never married.

President Fillmore and his wife riding in a horse-drawn carriage in Saratoga Springs, New York (1851).

# FAST FACTS

★ The Fillmore family enjoyed the new library created by their mom, Abigail Fillmore. She requested money from Congress to purchase all kinds of books. As a teacher, she was appalled that there was no White House library.

★ The Fillmores were the first White House family to enjoy a bathtub. It was made of mahogany and lined with zinc.

★ The family also enjoyed the White House's very first kitchen stove, installed during their administration.

★ The new library was located in the Oval Room on the second floor across from the Blue Room. Lots of children and first kids used the library to study and read. The library stayed in this location for many years.

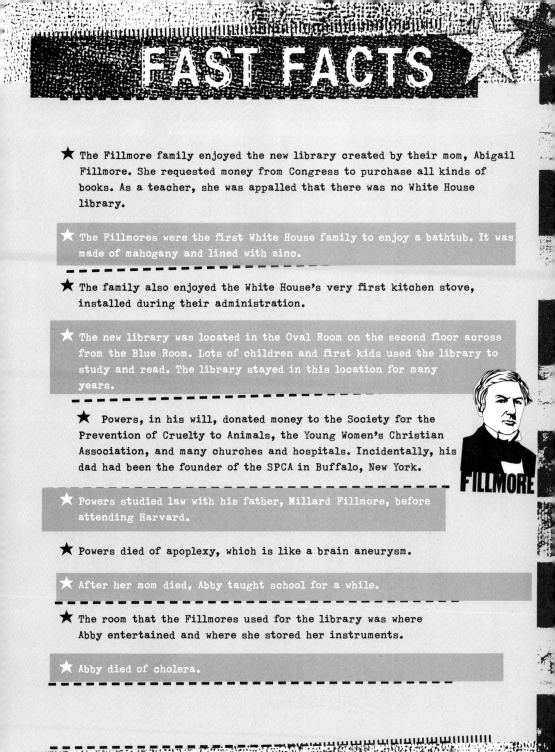

★ Powers, in his will, donated money to the Society for the Prevention of Cruelty to Animals, the Young Women's Christian Association, and many churches and hospitals. Incidentally, his dad had been the founder of the SPCA in Buffalo, New York.

FILLMORE

★ Powers studied law with his father, Millard Fillmore, before attending Harvard.

★ Powers died of apoplexy, which is like a brain aneurysm.

★ After her mom died, Abby taught school for a while.

★ The room that the Fillmores used for the library was where Abby entertained and where she stored her instruments.

★ Abby died of cholera.

President Pierce and his wife, Jane.

# The Pierces

*Franklin Pierce*
*(1853-1857)*

Franklin Pierce was considered charming and handsome. He was a decorated war hero and an amazing senator. Unfortunately, he has been called one of the worst presidents in history. After the deaths of his children, it was difficult for him to be an effective president. The administration of Franklin Pierce was one of the darkest times in the White House. His wife, Jane Means Appleton, usually wore black throughout her husband's administration and she never forgave him for becoming president.

## FRANKLIN PIERCE JR.

was born on February 2, 1836. He died three days after his birth.

# FRANK ROBERT PIERCE

came along on August 27, 1839. He was a happy boy but contracted typhus along with his younger brother and died at age four on November 14, 1843.

# BENJAMIN "BENNIE" PIERCE

was born on April 13, 1841. As a two-year-old, he caught typhus but lived. He was a happy-go-lucky eleven-year-old and excited by the fact that he would celebrate his twelfth birthday in the White House. Sadly, it was not meant to be. The Pierces were traveling home to Concord, New Hampshire, after a funeral. The train ride became a nightmare. The train derailed, and Bennie was crushed in front of his parents on January 16, 1853. President-elect Pierce and his wife were not hurt.

"You need no introduction to this house; it is your house and I am but the tenant for a time."
— Franklin Pierce

Mrs. Pierce and her son, Bennie (circa 1850).

# FAST FACTS

★ The very first night the Pierces moved into the White House, all the White House staff were gone due to a bitter winter snowstorm. President Pierce had to use a candle while climbing the stairs in search of a mattress.

★ President Franklin Pierce had the first bodyguard who was paid by the government.

★ Franklin Pierce had no official vice president his entire four years in office.

★ Franklin Pierce and his wife never recovered from the deaths of their children. President Pierce became an alcoholic, and Jane suffered from depression.

★ First lady Jane Pierce wrote notes to Bennie after his death.

★ Mrs. Pierce carried a small box containing locks of hair from all her sons. She also carried Bennie's Bible with her.

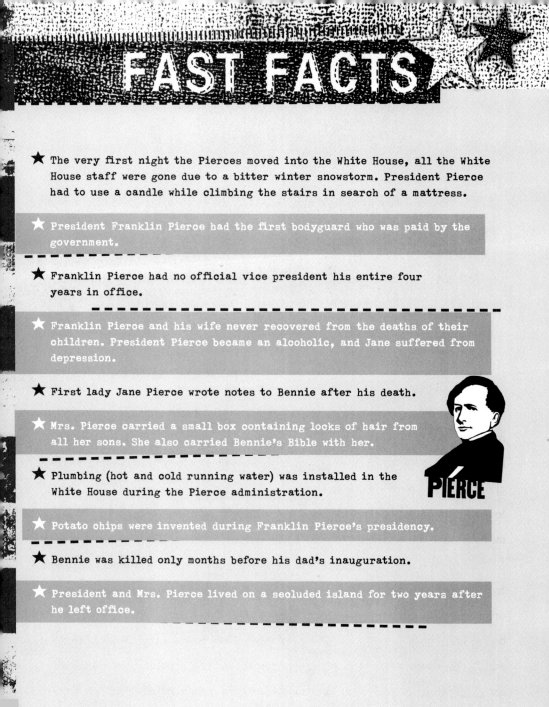

PIERCE

★ Plumbing (hot and cold running water) was installed in the White House during the Pierce administration.

★ Potato chips were invented during Franklin Pierce's presidency.

★ Bennie was killed only months before his dad's inauguration.

★ President and Mrs. Pierce lived on a secluded island for two years after he left office.

# The Buchanans

## James Buchanan
## (1857-1861)

ames Buchanan, the 15th president of the United States, is the only president to have the distinction of never marrying. Buchanan's niece served as White House hostess in the absence of a first lady. James Buchanan had actually raised his niece, Harriet Lane, since she was nine years of age. She was a brilliant hostess with poise and charm. Buchanan's cabinet was known to all of Washington as corrupt. They bribed, took bribes, and were distrusted by Congress. By the end of Buchanan's presidency, many states had seceded and the Confederate States of America had formed.

Because he never married, people might have assumed he was lonely. Bachelor James Buchanan had known love before, however. As a young man he had dated and planned to marry a young woman named Anne Coleman, but her parents broke the engagement. Soon afterward Anne died, and Buchanan swore that he would never marry. He couldn't have been too lonely with his best friend, Lara. Lara, a Newfoundland, was one of the biggest White House dogs in history. President Buchanan was very social in nature. He enjoyed having overnight guests at the White House. He once had so many visitors staying at the White House that he had to sleep on the floor in a hallway.

President Lincoln with his wife, Mary Todd, and sons, Tad, Willie, and Robert.

"Tell Tad the goats and father are very well — especially the goats!" — Abraham Lincoln, in a letter to his wife

# The Lincolns

*Abraham Lincoln (1861-1865)*

resident Abraham Lincoln and his wife, Mary Todd Lincoln, loved their children, but they also spoiled them rotten. Lincoln once said, "It is my pleasure that my children are free, happy, and unrestricted by parental tyranny." (Wow . . . would you want your parent to say that?) President Abraham Lincoln is often called America's best president. Both the president and his wife dealt with extreme joy and pain involving their children. This could be why they both suffered from depression. Mrs. Lincoln was diagnosed with mental illness toward the end of her life. Their children were their greatest joy but also their greatest sorrow.

## ROBERT TODD LINCOLN

was born on August 1, 1843. Robert was seventeen when his dad was elected president. He wouldn't move to the White House with his family because he was attending college. He first attended a prep school in New Hampshire to get him ready for Harvard, where he would graduate in 1864. His parents did not want him on the front lines of the Civil War, so his presidential father made an arrangement with General Grant. Robert was actually in Washington, D.C., with General Grant on the day his father was assassinated. Robert went on to become a successful lawyer and president of the famous Pullman Palace Car Company. Robert married and had a family and requested not to be buried with his famous first family upon his death. He is buried in Arlington National Cemetery, and the Lincoln family is buried in Springfield, Illinois. Robert Todd Lincoln was almost eighty-three years old when he died on July 26, 1926.

Robert Todd Lincoln (1853).

# EDWARD "EDDIE" BAKER LINCOLN

was next in line, born on March 10, 1846. Eddie was named after his dad's friend and colleague Edward D. Baker. Eddie did not survive childhood. He died at the age of three from tuberculosis on February 1, 1850.

# WILLIAM "WILLIE" WALLACE LINCOLN

is said to have been his parents' favorite child. He was born on December 21, 1850, in Springfield, Illinois. Willie was ten years old when his dad was elected president. He was a funny kid who enjoyed playing tricks on White House staff with his younger brother. Once Willie and his brother decided to have a circus on the roof of their home. They used their own pets as well as their neighborhood friends' pets for the animals in the circus. Another time, a famous painter was at the White House to paint their dad's presidential portrait. They waited until

Willie Lincoln at eleven years old (1862).

he left the room and proceeded to squeeze all the paint out of the tubes and onto the wall, floor, themselves, and anything else they considered a possible palette.

One night, Willie decided to take a ride on his favorite pony. There were two problems with this. The first problem was that it was late. Second, the weather was rainy

Mary Todd Lincoln's cousin, Captain Lockwood Todd, with Willie and Todd (1862).

and cold. Later, he and his little brother became ill. Tad recovered, but Willie did not. Willie died of typhoid fever at age eleven on February 20, 1862. Willie's mom never again entered the room that he died in or the East Room of the White House where his funeral took place.

# THOMAS "TAD" LINCOLN

looked like a tadpole when he was born, according to his dad, and the name Tad stuck! He was born on April 4, 1853. He was best friends with his older brother Willie

Tad Lincoln with his father (circa 1850s–1860s).

and was devastated by his death. Both the president and Mrs. Lincoln latched on to Tad after Willie's death. The White House staff was sympathetic at first, but soon became annoyed that Tad was permanently attached to his dad, sitting in on cabinet meetings and state dinners. Tad constantly tried to cheer up his depressed parents. While President Lincoln was making a speech for the Union victory in the Civil War in front of the White House, Tad decided to play a joke on his dad—he began waving a Confederate flag out the window. Tad fell apart when he heard that his dad had been assassinated. He died of diphtheria on July 15, 1871, at age eighteen.

President Lincoln, Mary Todd, Willie, and Robert.

Tad Lincoln riding a horse (circa 1860–1865).

Tad Lincoln wearing a Civil War uniform (1861).

# FAST FACTS

★ The Lincoln Memorial was completed fifty-seven years after President Lincoln's death.

★ The Lincoln family had an array of White House pets. Their turkey was named Tom (famously rescued before Thanksgiving). They had a pair of goats named Nanko and Nanny. Their horse was named Bob.

★ Robert Lincoln was in attendance at the dedication of the Lincoln Memorial on May 30, 1922. This was his very last public appearance.

★ Robert committed his mother to an insane asylum in 1875.

★ Robert was appointed to cabinet positions by Presidents Garfield and Arthur.

★ Robert rarely saw his dad because he was traveling and working so much as an attorney.

★ Mrs. Lincoln banned flowers from the White House after Willie's death because he loved them.

★ Mrs. Lincoln also banned Marine band concerts on the South Lawn of the White House because Willie loved them.

**ABE**

★ Willie enjoyed drawing and writing poetry. Some of his poetry was published in the newspaper.

★ Willie's body was removed from his resting place after President Lincoln's assassination. His body traveled with his dad's to Springfield, Illinois.

★ Tad had a speech impediment and lisp. Willie often translated for him.

★ Tad could barely read.

★ Tad once smeared ink on the telegraph desks at the White House.

★ Tad also was known for hammering nails into his father's desk.

# The Life and Times of the Lincoln Bed

Mary Todd Lincoln actually bought the Lincoln bed around 1861. It was put in the Prince of Wales Bedroom (northwest bedroom suite). No one knows if President Lincoln ever slept in it.

Julia Grant moved the Lincoln bed in 1869 to a small bedroom on the north portico side.

President Rutherford B. Hayes and Mrs. Hayes moved the famous bed to the State Bedroom. This room is now the president's personal study, adjacent to his private bedroom.

In 1901, the Lincoln bed was moved. It was placed in the southwest bedroom suite and used by President Theodore Roosevelt and his wife, Edith.

Nellie Taft had the Lincoln bed moved to storage in 1909.

Another Edith and her husband used the Lincoln bed in 1915. Edith and Woodrow Wilson had the famous bed placed back in the southwest bedroom suite, which was the president's bedroom.

Mrs. Harding made a shrine of sorts out of the famous bed. In 1921, she had it moved to the northwest suite along with Lincoln memorabilia and other things from that time period.

Calvin and Grace Coolidge used the Lincoln bed in 1921. They slept in the president's bedroom, which is sometimes called the southwest suite.

The Hoovers are responsible for naming the famous Lincoln Bedroom. In 1929, President and Mrs. Hoover had the famous bed moved back to the northwest suite and labeled it the Lincoln Bedroom.

FDR had the bed moved in 1933. One of his aides, Louis Howe, and his wife slept in the bed when it was moved to a small west bedroom. During FDR's tenure, the bed was moved back to the northwest suite and used by his daughter and her family.

The Lincoln bed was moved a final time in 1945 to the southeast suite (Blue Suite), which was then dubbed the Lincoln Bedroom during the Truman administration. It has remained in this suite to the present.

# The Andrew Johnsons

## Andrew Johnson
## (1865-1869)

Andrew Johnson was our 17th president and had five kids. This occupant of the highest office in the land had no schooling, and his wife taught him how to read. Even before his presidency, Mrs. Johnson had suffered from recurring tuberculosis, therefore leaving her daughters to serve as White House hostesses for their father. Following the assassination of President Lincoln, the Johnson family did not get to move into the White House right away. President Johnson set up his offices in the Treasury Department until Mrs. Lincoln moved out of the White House. Everything was worn and dirty. Soldiers had spat tobacco on floors and rugs; they had wandered through, day and night, and even slept on the furniture and in hallways. This family would experience a total White House restoration as well as an impeachment by Congress.

# MARTHA JOHNSON PATTERSON

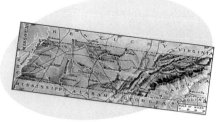

was born on October 25, 1828. Before her father was president, he was in the U.S. Congress. This called for travel back and forth to his home state of Tennessee. He would leave Martha in the care of President James K. Polk and his wife. They loved Martha and she gained the experience she would need, under the watchful eye of Mrs. Polk, to eventually refurbish the White House from top to bottom, and serve and entertain as hostess in place of her ailing mom. Martha eventually married Senator David Patterson from Tennessee and had two children by the time her father assumed the presidency. She lived nearly seventy-three years. She died on July 10, 1901.

# CHARLES JOHNSON

was born on February 19, 1830. He became a doctor and owned his own pharmacy. Charles served in the Civil War as a surgeon for the First Middle Tennessee Infantry. Though successful in his profession, he was not as successful in his personal life. He became an alcoholic and a drug addict and died in a riding accident on April 4, 1863. He was only thirty-three years old.

# MARY JOHNSON STOVER BROWN

was born on May 8, 1832. She was known to be a very cheerful person. She married a colonel in the Fourth Tennessee Union Infantry named Daniel Stover. The Stovers had three children together. The Civil War left Mary a widow, and she moved into the White House to help her sister, Martha, perform hostess duties for their mom. She eventually remarried and lived on a farm. She became estranged from her second husband, William Brown, but waited to divorce him until after her parents died . . . she didn't want to disappoint them. She died on April 19, 1883.

# ROBERT JOHNSON

was born on February 22, 1834. He was a colonel in the Union army and was loved by his men because he not only told them what to do but also fought right alongside them. The intensity of the war caused him to begin drinking heavily. Robert served briefly as a personal secretary to his father in the White House. After his dad lost the reelection, he moved back home to Tennessee and within weeks, on April 22, 1869, he was dead. Some historians believe that he drank himself to death. He lived to be thirty-five years old. Robert never married and had no children.

# ANDREW "FRANK" JOHNSON JR.

was born on August 6, 1852. He was twelve years old when his dad became president. He enjoyed living in the White House as a kid. He played with all of his nieces and nephews who lived there. He was a journalist by age twenty-one and started his own newspaper called the *Greenville Intelligencer*. It started off with a bang and had more than 800 subscribers, but soon failed because the only news he covered seemed to be tributes to his dad. He eventually married but only lived to age twenty-six. He died on March 12, 1879.

# FAST FACTS

★ The Johnson kids' mom, Eliza Johnson, only made an appearance at two White House events as first lady due to her poor health. One event was a dinner for the Queen of Hawaii and the other was a sixtieth birthday party for her husband.

★ President Johnson allowed his grandchildren to run freely in the White House, disturbing meetings and playing roughly. He would watch them take music lessons, visit them in their schoolroom in the White House, and play with them on the South Lawn.

★ Martha milked two Jersey cows each morning while at the White House. She loved cream and butter. She also allowed these cows to graze on the White House lawn to keep it well manicured.

★ Martha somehow convinced Congress to appropriate money to refurbish the ailing White House. It is said to have been more than $28,000.

★ Martha is hailed as one of the best hostesses in White House history. She hosted parties and entertained in such a way that it gave the Johnsons an elite reputation even though they considered themselves plain folk from Tennessee.

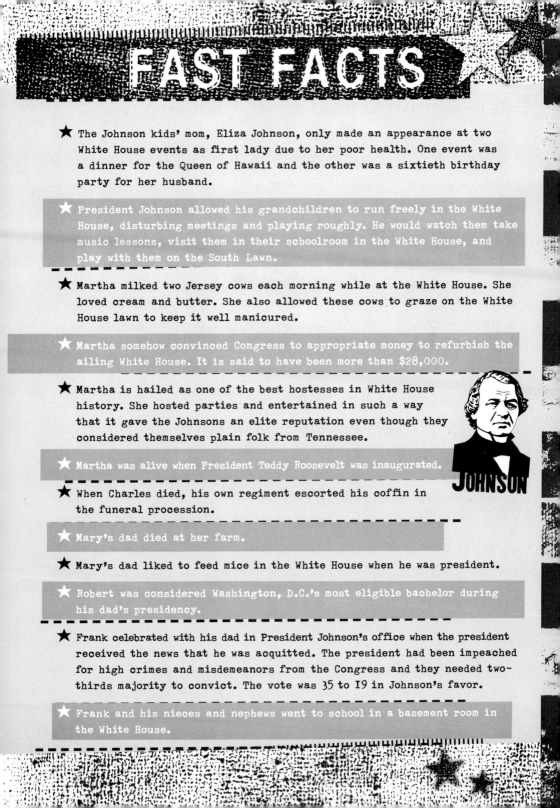

JOHNSON

★ Martha was alive when President Teddy Roosevelt was inaugurated.

★ When Charles died, his own regiment escorted his coffin in the funeral procession.

★ Mary's dad died at her farm.

★ Mary's dad liked to feed mice in the White House when he was president.

★ Robert was considered Washington, D.C.'s most eligible bachelor during his dad's presidency.

★ Frank celebrated with his dad in President Johnson's office when the president received the news that he was acquitted. The president had been impeached for high crimes and misdemeanors from the Congress and they needed two-thirds majority to convict. The vote was 35 to 19 in Johnson's favor.

★ Frank and his nieces and nephews went to school in a basement room in the White House.

"My life at the White House was like a bright and beautiful dream... quite the happiest period of my life."
— Julia Grant

# The Grants

## Ulysses S. Grant
## (1869-1877)

Ulysses S. Grant was a war hero and was treated like a superhero. He helped win the Civil War, became president, and wrote a bestselling book of memoirs that sustained his family financially after his death. He was a simple man, needing only cucumbers and syrup for his breakfast (GROSS!!!). He and his wife hosted many lavish dinners in the White House. Mrs. Grant loved being a first lady and brought the younger Grant kids with them to the White House. This family had a lot of fun together. Ulysses had a billiard room added to the White House while he lived there. The Grant family played games and pool with one another and with friends until the wee hours of the morning. The new room got lots of use during this administration.

## FREDRICK "FRED" DENT GRANT

was born on May 30, 1850, and he aspired to be just like his dad. By the time he was thirteen, he had more military experience than a lot of grown men because he had accompanied his dad as the commander of the Union army at Vicksburg. He wanted a military career so badly that he began by entering West Point and graduating there near the bottom of the class. Fred married Ida Maria Honoré while his dad was in office. Together they had two children. He spent time in the army and then accepted President Benjamin Harrison's appointment as minister to Austria. He also served as the New York City police commissioner and attained the second highest military ranking in the United States, finishing his career as a major general. He died of cancer on April 11, 1912. He was sixty-one years of age.

Frederick Grant (circa 1862).

## ULYSSES "BUCK" SIMPSON GRANT JR.

was his famous father's namesake. He was born on July 22, 1852. He graduated from Harvard after studying at Phillips Exeter Academy, as well as a university in Germany. He also studied at Columbia Law School. He passed the bar but chose to be his father's personal secretary during the White House years. Buck met Josephine Chaffee, and they later married. They would have five kids together in total. His new wife gave him a large sum of money that he used to open a New York banking and brokerage partnership. Buck was soon a financial success and had quadrupled his original investment. After some illegal business dealings, he was shut down. His wife died, and he remarried a young widow half his age and built the U. S. Grant hotel in California. He died on September 26, 1929, at age seventy-seven.

Ulysses Grant Jr. (1862).

# ELLEN "NELLIE" WRENSHALL GRANT SARTORIS JONES

was the Grants' only daughter. She was born on July 4, 1855. Nellie was thirteen years old when she moved into the White House as a first kid. She was considered hip, and all of Washington's teenagers wanted to be like her. When Nellie turned eighteen, she was engaged to be married to Algernon Sartoris. Hers was one of the most lavish weddings in White House history. A

Nellie Grant (1867).

Methodist minister married Nellie and her husband in the White House East Room. There were gifts from citizens all over the country and dignitaries all over the world. All the wedding guests were treated to a huge feast in the State Dining Room. After getting a divorce, she found love again with her childhood sweetheart, but months after their marriage, she became sick and was paralyzed. She lived this way for ten years and died at age sixty-seven on August 30, 1922.

Jesse Grant with his parents (1872).

# JESSE ROOT GRANT

was the baby of the Grant family. Born on February 6, 1858, he was just ten when his dad was elected president. The White House was his playground. Life in the White House was freedom for Jesse and Nellie. Jesse had many neighborhood friends who visited often. They found much to do in the vacant lot by the White House, and they would play hide-and-seek on the ground floor. Jesse was given a special gift from a family friend. It was a small, high-powered telescope that he used on the White House roof at night. Stargazing bonded him with his dad. On clear nights, they could be found on the roof for hours. Jesse was never the politician his father had hoped he would be. In college, he declared himself a Democrat (President Grant was a Republican) and he graduated from Cornell with an engineering degree. He married and had two kids but divorced. He later remarried, and died when he was seventy-six years old on June 8, 1934.

The Grant family on the porch of their house (1880).

Nellie and Jesse Grant (1862).

President Grant, seated, with his wife and children.

# FAST FACTS

- First lady Julia Grant's father, Fredrick Dent, lived with the Grants in the White House. He was the first "first grandpa" to live there.

- Grandpa Dent died in the White House at the age of eighty-seven.

- Fred married while his dad was president, but the wedding did not take place in the White House.

- First lady Julia Grant hosted a reception for her new granddaughter to be introduced to the world. This was Fred's first child.

- Fred entered West Point at age sixteen.

- Fred died of throat cancer, just like his father.

- Fred had always wanted to die a war hero. At his death, he was given full military honors.

GRANT

- Fred's funeral was widely attended. One of the more well-known attendees was Vice President William Howard Taft.

- Buck ran for the U.S. Senate representing California, but his plans were crushed when it was discovered that he was bribing people to vote for him.

- Nellie was the first teenage daughter in the White House since Abby Fillmore.

- First dad Ulysses S. Grant guessed that Jesse's secret club, known as the K.F.R. Society, stood for Kick, Fight, and Run. Jesse would never confirm or deny.

- Jesse would ride his bike right into lines of office seekers at the White House.

- Jesse loved to wrestle.

- Jesse never really settled down as a family man. During his first marriage, he traveled constantly and spent little time at home.

- Jesse's book, *In the Days of My Father, General Grant*, was published in 1925.

# The Hayeses

President Hayes with his wife, Lucy (circa 1870s–1880s).

*Rutherford B. Hayes (1877-1881)*

Rutherford B. Hayes and his wife, "Lemonade" Lucy, were the heads of one of the most colorful and interesting families to ever inhabit the White House. They were extremely close to each other as well as their children. They were bonded perhaps by the tragedy of losing three young sons in infancy. Some say they were religiously observant, beginning each day in prayer together, reading the Bible, and singing hymns. During this administration there would be no pool playing, smoking, drinking, or card playing. First Lady Lucy Hayes had former president Grant's billiard table sent to the White House basement, and banned all alcohol from the premises as well. The White House only served lemonade. Despite all the rules, they did dance, sing, and entertain. They also had the first White House telephone. Actually, they used one of the very first phones anywhere. Their telephone number was easy for the entire family to remember . . . it was "1."

# BIRCHARD "BIRCH" AUSTIN HAYES

was born on November 4, 1853. He was a Harvard law student when his father became president. His dad's advice to him was always simply, "Do the right thing, be kind, love your family." Birch went on to open his own law practice specializing in tax and real estate law. He was a successful attorney for twenty-six years who married Mary Sherman and had four kids. He lived to be seventy-two years old. He died on January 24, 1926.

# JAMES WEBB COOK HAYES

dropped the James and was known forever as Webb Cook Hayes. He was born on March 20, 1856. When his dad was elected president, Webb eagerly became his confidential secretary and guard. He eventually became a wealthy and respected businessman. Webb was searching for his next adventure when he decided to try his hand at fighting. Fighting in wars became his new passion. He fought in the Spanish-American War, the Boxer Rebellion, and with British and French brigades. He eventually ended up in the U.S. Army as a major during World War I. He did marry but had no children and died at the ripe old age of seventy-eight on July 26, 1934.

# RUTHERFORD "RUDDY" PLATT HAYES

Webb and Ruddy Hayes with their father.

was born on June 24, 1858. He was tall and mild-mannered. Ruddy was given a position on the board of trustees for his uncle's library. By being involved in the operation of the library, he discovered what would eventually become his vocation and passion. He served as secretary, vice president, and acting president of the American Library Association (ALA), which is alive and well today. He also created a way for rural communities to experience having a library if they could not afford to build one. Ruddy created mobile libraries or book wagons (with the later invention of motorized cars, this concept continued as the popular bookmobiles). These mobile libraries would travel from town to town, allowing citizens to check out books, read, and expand their horizons. He married his cousin, Lucy Hayes Platt, and had three kids. Ruddy died on July 31, 1927.

Lucy Hayes with Carrie Paulding Davis (left), the daughter of a friend, Scott, and Fanny.

## JOSEPH THOMPSON HAYES

arrived in time for Christmas on December 21, 1861. The Civil War had just begun, and his dad was an officer. The family was going to pack up and meet Dad in his camp location during the war so that he could see the baby. However, tragedy struck and the meeting became a funeral rather than an introduction. Baby Joseph died of dysentery at eighteen months on June 24, 1863.

## GEORGE CROOK HAYES

was born on September 29, 1864. He was named after General George Crook, a friend of his father's. Sadly, he would not live to celebrate his second birthday. He died on May 24, 1866.

## FANNY HAYES SMITH

was born on September 2, 1867. She would bring joy and femininity to a house full of men. She was named after her dad's sister. Fanny was nine years old when her dad entered the White House. Ruddy was her best friend during her White House years.

Fanny and her brother often received gifts from their parents as well as other leaders and dignitaries. Of all the gifts she received, dollhouses were her favorite. She had so many that the White House cleaning staff complained that they were everywhere. Fanny enjoyed her time in the White House and later served as her father's traveling companion and hostess, following the death of her mom. After the death of her father, she married and had one child. When her husband died, she changed her name back to Hayes. She died on March 19, 1950, when she was eighty-two years old.

## SCOTT RUSSELL HAYES

was born on February 8, 1871. Scott was fun-loving and good-natured, and only six years old when he took up residence in the White House. One of Scott's favorite things while in the White House was a tradition that his mom and dad reinstated, the famous Easter Egg Roll. It had begun at the Capitol but had been canceled because it ruined the grass and left cracked shells littered everywhere. Rutherford and Lucy Hayes reinstated the famous Easter fun on the White House lawn. They rode horses for fun and loved to play games like hide-and-seek because the White House offered a vast amount of possibilities for this game. When Scott grew up, he had no interest in politics. He married but had no children and died of a brain tumor at age fifty-two on May 6, 1923.

The Hayes family with friends in their library, today's yellow Oval Room in the White House.

## MANNING FORCE HAYES

was the last of the Hayes children, born on August 1, 1873. Manning was named for the son of one of his dad's friends. Unfortunately, he only lived for one year and died on August 28, 1874.

# FAST FACTS

★ The Hayes family had the very first Siamese cat in America.

★ Rutherford and Lucy Hayes were the wealthiest first family to live in the White House up to that time.

★ Lucy Hayes was the first, first lady to have graduated from college.

★ Hayes was one of three presidents to keep a personal diary while in the White House rather than an official one. The others were John Quincy Adams and James K. Polk.

★ Birch was used to moving around a lot the first ten years of his life because his dad was in the army.

★ When his father died, Webb was at his side.

★ Webb was the only Hayes child to work for his dad in the White House.

★ Webb was awarded a Congressional Medal of Honor for his war action in the Philippines.

★ Webb created the first presidential library in his dad's memory. It is located in Fremont, Ohio.

HAYES

★ Ruddy, responsible for cofounding the ALA, also created the concept of children's reading rooms within libraries. This meant kids' books, and kid-size tables and chairs.

★ Fanny and Scott were fascinated by their father's telephone in the White House.

★ Fanny and Scott would beg visiting officials to the White House to play hide-and-seek.

★ Scott hooked up a cart to his pet goat and would ride around the grounds of the White House.

★ Scott became a railroad executive as a grown-up.

President Garfield
and his family.

# The Garfields

*James A. Garfield*
*(1881)*

J ames Garfield was inaugurated as the 20th president of the United States. First lady Lucretia Garfield came down with malaria. The family decided to send her back to their home in New Jersey to recuperate and regain her strength. The day finally arrived when first kids Hal and Jim would travel with their famous father by train to New England to see their father's alma mater, Williams College. Suddenly, the Garfield family plans were altered forever. Harry and Jim witnessed the shooting of their father by a deranged and disgruntled office seeker named Charles Guiteau. The president was returned to the White House for treatment. There was a team of physicians waiting to extract the bullets . . . if they could find them. This was before the days of X-rays, so it was almost impossible. Then Alexander Graham Bell offered his services by bringing one of his inventions to help locate the bullets. It was a metal detector of sorts, but it could not locate the lodged bullet because Garfield was lying on a bed of metal springs. Meanwhile, the surgeons probed and poked. Their hands and the environment were not sterile, which was a more serious threat than any bullet.

Garfield was later moved by train, on tracks lined with straw for his comfort, to reunite with his family in New Jersey. Unfortunately, he died soon after the reunion, on September 19, 1881.

The Garfield children (circa 1881).

# ELIZA "TROT" ARABELLA GARFIELD

was lovingly called Trot by her family. She was born on July 3, 1860. Her joyous life was cut short by diphtheria. She was only three years old when she died on December 3, 1863.

# HARRY "HAL" AUGUSTUS GARFIELD

was born on October 11, 1863. Hal was a war baby, born at the height of the Civil War. He eventually became a professor at Williams College and Princeton. He was hired by a later president, Woodrow Wilson, to chair the price committee of the U.S. Food Administration. Later, Wilson made him the U.S. fuel administrator. After finishing these assignments, Hal returned to lead his alma mater, Williams College, as its president. He married Belle Hartford Mason and together they raised four children. He died on December 12, 1942, at age seventy-nine.

# JAMES "JIM" RUDOLF GARFIELD

was born on October 17, 1865. Jim was sixteen years old when his family moved into the White House. Before his 30th birthday, he was elected to the state senate of Ohio. Soon, he was appointed by President McKinley to a post in the Department of Commerce and Labor. President Roosevelt appointed him to a cabinet position as Secretary of the Interior, and he helped establish the Bull Moose Party. Later he assisted President Herbert Hoover in a failed effort for reelection. He was married and had four children. He lived to be eighty-four years old and died on March 24, 1950.

## MARY "MOLLY" GARFIELD STANLEY-BROWN

Molly Garfield and her father.

was born on January 16, 1867. Molly was fourteen when her family moved into the White House. Her love story would begin here. President Garfield's private secretary was Joseph Stanley-Brown. After her dad died, Molly and Joseph corresponded regularly, and developed a strong relationship. They were eventually married and had three children, and both lived to celebrate their fiftieth wedding anniversary. Molly died on December 30, 1947, at age eighty.

## IRVIN MCDOWELL GARFIELD

was born on August 3, 1870. At age ten, the White House seemed like an amusement park just for him. The staff dubbed him "the terror of the White House." He loved to ride his bike down the formal staircase, often taking out historic chunks of trim and paint on his way down and into the East Room. He only got to stay in the White House about a year before moving with his sick mom to New Jersey for her to recover. He went on to law school but chose to practice in Boston rather than Ohio like his older brothers. He married Susan Emmons and had three children. Irvin lived until July 19, 1951. He was eighty years old when he died.

The Garfield family in Ohio (circa 1881).

## ABRAM GARFIELD

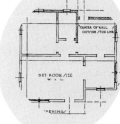

was named after his dad, James Abram Garfield. He was born on November 21, 1872. He was only eight years old when his dad became president. He, too, followed his brothers to Williams College, but did not go into law; he chose architecture instead. He opened his own firm in Cleveland, Ohio, and became a committee chairman for the American Institute of Architecture. President Roosevelt appointed Abram to the National Council of Fine Arts in 1909, and in 1925 President Coolidge named him to serve on the National Fine Arts Commission. He was married twice and had two children. He lived to the age of eighty-five. He died on October 16, 1958.

## EDWARD GARFIELD

was born on Christmas Day in 1874. He didn't get to know his new family very well because he died on October 25, 1876, of whooping cough, just twenty-two months after his birth.

# FAST FACTS

★ President Garfield had little time for his kids because of his busy job at the White House. He was so strict about their education that they all called him General.

★ The Garfield kids complained when they didn't eat with their dad for two weeks straight while in the White House.

★ The Garfields purchased their first family home for less than $850.

★ President Garfield came from a very modest background. He worked as a carpenter and janitor to support himself in college. He became the yougest brigadier general in the Union army and a House minority leader.

★ First Lady Lucretia Garfield was the first, first lady to take inventory of the things in the White House.

★ More than $300,000 worth of donations were sent to the Garfield family following the death of President Garfield.

GARFIELD

★ Robert Lincoln was in Washington when his dad was assassinated. He was also in Washington when Garfield was assassinated and he was in town again when President McKinley was assassinated.

★ Harry and his brother Jim had a private tutor while in the White House. They studied in a small hideaway upstairs in preparation for college.

★ Harry, Jim, and President Garfield often had wrestling matches and pillow fights in the White House.

★ Harry and Jim remained with their dad at the White House after he was shot, until he was taken back to New Jersey.

★ Molly once gave a tea party in the White House, and all of her friends came, including Fanny Hayes, the former president's daughter.

★ Molly played piano and loved to entertain.

★ Irvin and Abram were often more interested in riding their bikes down the White House halls than studying.

# The Arthurs

President Arthur
and his wife, Ellen.

*Chester A. Arthur*
*(1881-1885)*

hester Arthur took one look at the White House and refused to live there. The septic system was failing; the basement was crumbling and giving way. All of the servants' quarters were in poor condition. In the White House kitchen, all of the paint on the ceiling was flaking and many times would fall right into the food. Arthur wanted to build a new mansion, but he couldn't convince anyone of this plan. Congress agreed to remodel the White House and gave Arthur more than $30,000. With this, he had the White House restored to "American royalty" status, hiring a famous New York designer named Louis Tiffany to help with the huge task. Many of the stars and eagle motifs from the Arthurs' refurbishment are in use today at the White House. He also hired a French gourmet chef to take over the White House kitchen after they fixed all of the chipping paint.

## WILLIAM LEWIS ARTHUR

was born while his dad was in the military on December 10, 1860. He died of convulsions at the age of two, on July 7, 1863.

# CHESTER ALAN ARTHUR II

was born on July 25, 1864, bringing back some joy to the Arthur household. Known as Alan, he was a student at Princeton when his dad became president. He would constantly entertain and impress his friends and dates by taking them to the White House for weekends. He often used his dad's presidential carriage to parade them around Washington in luxury. Alan loved to entertain on his dad's yacht as well. When his dad died, Alan destroyed most of President Arthur's presidential papers like his father had instructed him to do. He traveled to Europe to mourn and regroup and rarely came back. He was expected to run his dad's New York law firm, but never completed law school. He became friends and associates with royalty in Europe and lived there almost until his death. After two marriages and one child, he died at the age of seventy-three on July 17, 1937.

# ELLEN "NELLIE" HERNDON ARTHUR PINKERTON

was the princess of the Arthur clan. She was born on November 21, 1871. Nellie was nine years old when her dad became the president. She loved the White House and attended most of the receptions and special events held there during her dad's time in office. President Arthur would not allow the press to photograph Nellie or her brother ever. Chester Arthur also would not allow any press interviews with his kids. He tried to maintain his private life. Nellie's favorite thing to do in the White House was to play on a new invention, the elevator, which had been installed in the renovated Executive Mansion. She grew up and married Charles Pinkerton. She died on September 6, 1915, from complications in surgery (blood transfusions). Nellie lived to be forty-three years old.

# FAST FACTS

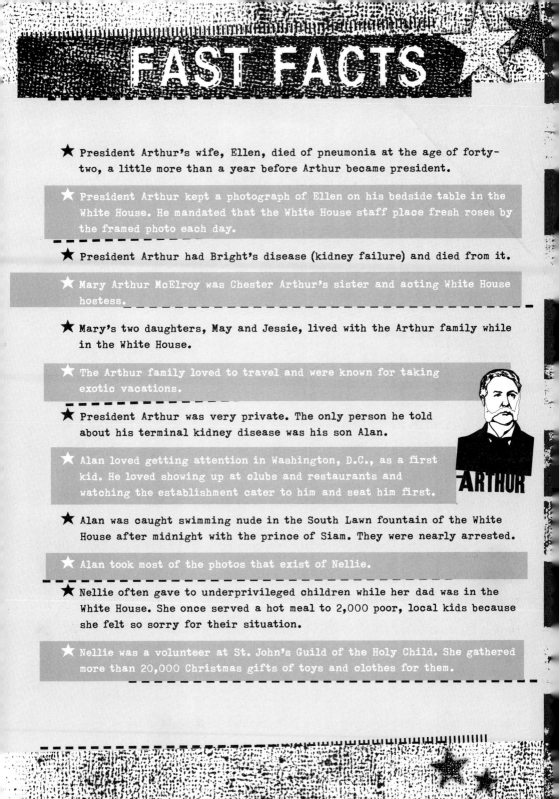

★ President Arthur's wife, Ellen, died of pneumonia at the age of forty-two, a little more than a year before Arthur became president.

★ President Arthur kept a photograph of Ellen on his bedside table in the White House. He mandated that the White House staff place fresh roses by the framed photo each day.

★ President Arthur had Bright's disease (kidney failure) and died from it.

★ Mary Arthur McElroy was Chester Arthur's sister and acting White House hostess.

★ Mary's two daughters, May and Jessie, lived with the Arthur family while in the White House.

★ The Arthur family loved to travel and were known for taking exotic vacations.

★ President Arthur was very private. The only person he told about his terminal kidney disease was his son Alan.

★ Alan loved getting attention in Washington, D.C., as a first kid. He loved showing up at clubs and restaurants and watching the establishment cater to him and seat him first.

ARTHUR

★ Alan was caught swimming nude in the South Lawn fountain of the White House after midnight with the prince of Siam. They were nearly arrested.

★ Alan took most of the photos that exist of Nellie.

★ Nellie often gave to underprivileged children while her dad was in the White House. She once served a hot meal to 2,000 poor, local kids because she felt so sorry for their situation.

★ Nellie was a volunteer at St. John's Guild of the Holy Child. She gathered more than 20,000 Christmas gifts of toys and clothes for them.

President Cleveland and family (from left to right), Esther, Francis, wife Frances, Marion, and Richard (circa 1904–1908).

"My mother did not want us to grow up dwelling on the fact that we had been White House children. She trained us for living on our own account."
— Marion Cleveland

# The Clevelands

## Grover Cleveland
### (1885-1889 + 1893-1897)

President Grover Cleveland entered the White House as a bachelor. A year into his term as the 22nd president of the United States, he did something no other president had done yet. Grover Cleveland was the first U.S. president to marry in the White House. His love story is an unusual one. Grover Cleveland was a partner in a law firm with Oscar Folsom. Cleveland adored the Folsom children and never realized that Frances Folsom, twenty-seven years younger than him, would become his wife, first lady, and mother of his children. They were married in the East Room of the White House in June 1886 in a small private ceremony. Frances was the youngest first lady in U.S. history. The first couple was so popular that they had to buy a retreat home to get away to so that they could have some privacy. Their second home was known as Red Top. They would go on to have the first child of a president to be born in the White House (Esther Cleveland) and the first, first couple to hold office for two nonconsecutive terms. After losing the election to Benjamin Harrison, Grover Cleveland left the White House, but in four years returned as the 24th president of the United States.

90

# RUTH CLEVELAND

was born during the four-year hiatus between her father's two administrations on October 3, 1891. Ruth eventually became America's sweetheart. Because the press reported on her so often, she was nicknamed Baby Ruth. Her blond hair and cute disposition were irresistible to America. At age twelve, Ruth developed diphtheria. Though hers was not a serious case, the diphtheria

Portrait of President Cleveland with his wife and child.

weakened Ruth's heart, and she died on January 7, 1904. America mourned, along with her family, and newspapers were filled with her story. Seventeen years after her death, the Curtiss Candy Company supposedly changed the name of their popular Candy Cake to Baby Ruth in a tribute to the sweet little girl who died so young.

# ESTHER CLEVELAND BOSANQUET

was the first, first kid born in the White House on September 9, 1893. History does not go into detail on her education and upbringing other than her marrying into British society. She married Captain William Sydney Bence Bosanquet in Westminster Abbey in 1918. They had two children whom they raised in Great Britain. Esther returned briefly to the United States after her husband died, and she lived in New Hampshire until she died at the age of eighty-six on June 26, 1980.

# MARION CLEVELAND DELL AMEN

was born at the Cleveland's summer home on July 7, 1895. Her dad was still commander in chief when she arrived. History records Marion using her education and talents in the areas of fund-raising, volunteering, advocacy, and charity. Marion married William Stanley Dell and had a daughter. They divorced; then she married John Harlan Amen, New York City's special assistant to the U.S. attorney. Marion was

committed to promoting and empowering girls within the Girl Scouts of America. She worked with this organization for many years until her retirement. She died on June 18, 1977, and lived to be almost eighty-two years old.

Baby Marion with Mrs. Cleveland (1896).

# RICHARD "DICK" FOLSOM CLEVELAND

was born on October 28, 1897. Dick came into the Cleveland family while his dad was teaching at Princeton University. He attended Phillips Exeter Academy before going on to Princeton and ultimately Harvard Law School. Dick was athletic and popular during his college years. He served as an officer in the U.S. Marines in World War I, interrupting his college education. He returned and obtained his degrees and went on to a law career in Baltimore, Maryland. Dick married twice and had six children. He died on January 10, 1974, at the age of seventy-six.

# FRANCIS GROVER CLEVELAND

was born on July 18, 1903. He would be only years old when his famous father died. His mom remarried, and she and her new husband raised Francis. He attended Phillips Exeter Academy like his older brother and eventually graduated from Harvard. He went on to teach drama at a private school and even acted briefly in New York. He married Alice Erdman and had one child. He died in 1995, living to be ninety-two years old.

Francis with his father and dog, Hector (circa 1907).

# FAST FACTS

★ Grover Cleveland spent hours on the job. He would often be at his desk until two a.m. He actually worked right up until minutes before his White House wedding.

★ The Clevelands had a dog, mockingbirds, and several canaries.

★ Hector, the Cleveland family dog, ate a rotten egg during the famous Easter Egg Roll that made him very sick.

★ The American people were so infatuated with the Cleveland children, they would surround the baby strollers, take souvenirs, and touch the babies.

CLEVELAND

★ The Cleveland wedding in the White House was small and elegant. There were no bridesmaids or groomsmen. President Cleveland had invited only close friends, family, and cabinet members and their wives.

★ The Cleveland kids were adored by the White House staff.

★ White House visitors were constantly trying to snip locks of Ruth's hair when they visited the Executive Mansion.

★ The press was fascinated with Esther and her sisters and constantly tried to photograph them while they were in the White House.

★ There was a song written for President Cleveland's second daughter called "Esther's Lullaby."

★ President Cleveland used Marion to press a button in the White House that symbolized the beginning of the Cotton Fair in Atlanta.

★ Francis was born when his father was sixty-six years old.

# First Dads Who Served Two Full Terms in Office

GEORGE WASHINGTON

THOMAS JEFFERSON

JAMES MADISON

JAMES MONROE

ANDREW JACKSON

ULYSSES S. GRANT

GROVER CLEVELAND

(nonconsecutive terms — 22nd and 24th administrations)

WOODROW WILSON

FRANKLIN D. ROOSEVELT

DWIGHT D. EISENHOWER

RONALD REAGAN

WILLIAM J. CLINTON

GEORGE W. BUSH

# The Benjamin Harrisons

## Benjamin Harrison
## (1889-1893)

enjamin Harrison moved into the White House as the 23rd president of the United States. However, he was also the grandson of the ninth president of the United States, William Henry Harrison. The Harrison children were grown-ups and had their own families when their dad took office. The Harrison White House was filled with the laughter of grandchildren. President Benjamin Harrison's most popular grandchild seemed to be Benjamin McKee, also known as Baby McKee. The press photographed Baby McKee leading the Marine band, signing papers, and crawling into cabinet meetings. First Lady Caroline Harrison was not satisfied with all the work that had been done previously on the White House and got Congress to give her $35,000 to refurbish and upgrade the mansion. Electricity was installed in the White House during the Benjamin Harrisons' stay and they were deathly afraid of it, so much so that they left the lights on for weeks because they were afraid to touch the switches to turn them off. Mrs. Harrison got very sick and became the second first lady to die in the White House (first was John Tyler's first wife). President Harrison eventually married his widowed niece, Mary Scott Lord Dimmick.

# RUSSELL BENJAMIN HARRISON

was born in Oxford, Ohio, on August 12, 1854. He was six when the Civil War began. He married the daughter of Nebraska senator Alvin Saunders. Mary Angeline Saunders and Russell had two kids together. Russell went on to become U.S. treasurer and would develop a close friendship with another influential politician, Teddy Roosevelt. He eventually became his father's official aide and secretary during his presidency. Russell died on December 13, 1936, at the age of eighty-two.

# MARY SCOTT HARRISON MCKEE

was born April 3, 1858. Mary went to various private schools and attended college. She married James Robert McKee in Indiana. She had two children, Benjamin and Mary Lodge McKee. Her son, Benjamin, or Baby McKee, became the White House prince. She was a dedicated wife and mother who died of cancer at the age of seventy-two on October 28, 1930.

Mary with her father and son, Baby McKee (circa 1896 or later).

# ELIZABETH HARRISON WALKER

was born on February 21, 1897, to Benjamin Harrison and Mary Scott Lord Dimmick. She was known as the stepsister. She was not well received by her half brother and sister because they disagreed with the marriage of their father to Mary. Elizabeth was admitted to both the New York and Indiana state bars before the age of 23. She married James Blaine Walker, who was the grand-nephew of Benjamin Harrison's secretary of state. She was considered one of the predominate women leading the feminist movement of the mid-20th century. She had two children. Elizabeth died on December 26, 1955, at the age of fifty-eight.

# FAST FACTS

★ President Benjamin Harrison once hosted a birthday party for his grandson Baby McKee, who was turning four years old. Fourteen guests were invited into the Blue Room where fifteen high chairs were placed around the dining table. The menu was ground-up food (biscuits and bouillon), cake, and ice cream. The Marine band supplied the music.

★ Benjamin Harrison and his family loved to duck hunt.

★ President Benjamin Harrison had a reputation for spending little time in the office, often finishing by noon.

★ During the rainy inauguration parade of President Benjamin Harrison, his son Russell and his brother-in-law decided to seek the dry asylum of the White House instead.

★ Russell and his wife were accused of receiving a federal salary for doing nothing. They were constantly scrutinized for their financial dealings.

★ Her friends and family often called Mary, Mamie.

★ Mary campaigned with her dad for reelection. He was unsuccessful.

★ Elizabeth started a monthly newsletter for women called Cues on the News. This newsletter included investment tips and economic advice for women.

★ Elizabeth's dad died when she was four years old.

★ Elizabeth was a first kid but never got to live in the White House.

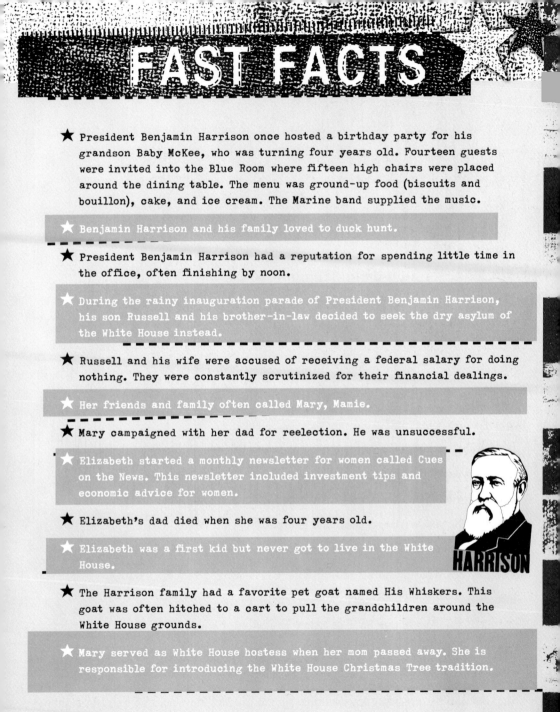

HARRISON

★ The Harrison family had a favorite pet goat named His Whiskers. This goat was often hitched to a cart to pull the grandchildren around the White House grounds.

★ Mary served as White House hostess when her mom passed away. She is responsible for introducing the White House Christmas Tree tradition.

President McKinley with his wife, Ida (circa 1900).

# The McKinleys

## William McKinley (1897-1901)

Carnations and roses were significant during William McKinley's administration. Why carnations and roses? It seemed that the McKinleys were obsessed with flowers. Mrs. McKinley hated yellow. In fact, she had all of the yellow roses dug up and removed from the White House grounds. President McKinley, on the other hand, didn't hate any color but preferred red carnations. He wore a red carnation in his lapel for good luck each and every day. While attending the Pan American Exposition in Buffalo, New York, McKinley noticed a young girl waiting to shake his hand. He bent down, shook her hand, and gave her his "lucky" red carnation. Within minutes, shots rang out and the president lay bleeding on the ground. He would be dead in eight days, after serving 1,654 days in office. The McKinleys had two daughters.

# KATHERINE "KATIE" MCKINLEY

was born in 1871. Historians argue whether December 15 or 25, 1871, was her official birthday. Katie amazed both her parents and was the apple of her dad's eye. Unfortunately, she would not have the opportunity to grow into adulthood. Katie died of typhoid fever on June 25, 1875, before her dad became commander in chief.

# IDA MCKINLEY

was born on April 1, 1873. She was named for her mother. Mrs. McKinley suffered through a very difficult childbirth with her second child. Ida's birth left her with many health problems that would last through the rest of her life. Little Ida was sickly at birth and died within six months on August 22, 1873. The McKinleys would enter the White House without children and with broken hearts.

Mr. and Mrs. McKinley (1890).

# FAST FACTS

★ The McKinleys had a pet parrot that could whistle "Yankee Doodle."

★ President McKinley would take his grieving wife on carriage rides to try and lift her spirits while in the White House.

★ When President McKinley was out of town on business, he would write his wife a daily letter.

★ The McKinleys once served a meal in the White House that consisted of 71 courses.

★ When baby Ida died, Mrs. McKinley would not allow President McKinley and her other daughter, Katie, to hug each other. She only wanted the president and her daughter to hug her! (She was suffering from a psychological breakdown.)

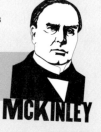

★ First Lady Ida McKinley had premonitions and dreams of her firstborn daughter, Katie, dying before they came true.

★ Mrs. McKinley suffered seizures all her life.

**MCKINLEY**

★ The McKinley family often gathered in the Blue Room of the White House for Sunday evening hymn singing. Sometimes they invited friends.

★ Pepsi was first invented in 1893. It was originally called "Brad's drink," but was renamed "Pepsi Cola" during President McKinley's term in 1898.

★ President McKinley was the first president ever to have his inauguration filmed.

★ When President McKinley collapsed after being shot by an assassins bullet, he was very concerned how his wife would take the news. He told his aides to be careful how they told her.

# *First Family Retreats*

John Adams, John Quincy Adams — *Peacefield*, later named *Old House*, Quincy, Massachusetts

Thomas Jefferson — *Monticello*, Charlottesville, Virginia

James Madison — *Montpelier*, Virginia

James Monroe — *Oak Hill*, Virginia

Andrew Jackson — *Hermitage*, Tennessee

Grover Cleveland — *Gray Gables*, Cape Cod, Massachusetts

William McKinley — Mom's home and his own home in Canton, Ohio

Teddy Roosevelt — *Sagamore Hill*, New York

Calvin Coolidge — family farm, Plymouth Notch, Vermont

Franklin D. Roosevelt — *Springwood*, Hyde Park, New York

Harry Truman — *Wallace Mansion*, Missouri

Dwight D. Eisenhower — Mamie's mother's home in Denver, Colorado; Eisenhower farm, Gettysburg, Pennsylvania

John F. Kennedy — *Kennedy Compound*, Hyannis, Massachusetts

Lyndon B. Johnson — *LBJ Ranch*, Johnson City, Texas

Richard M. Nixon — *La Casa Pacifica*, San Clemente, California

Jimmy Carter — Carter family farm, Plains, Georgia

Ronald Reagan — *Rancho del Cielo*, Santa Barbara, California

George H. W. Bush — *Walker's Point*, Kennebunkport, Maine

George W. Bush — his ranch in Crawford, Texas

President Roosevelt, Archie, Ted, Alice, Kermit, Edith (wife), and Ethel (1895).

"I can run the country, or I can control Alice. I cannot possibly do both!"
— Theodore Roosevelt

# The Teddy Roosevelts

## Theodore Roosevelt (1901-1909)

Theodore Roosevelt entered the White House as the youngest president in U.S. history. He was forty-two years old and assumed office because of the death of President William McKinley. John F. Kennedy would later become the youngest elected president in history. Roosevelt met his first wife Alice Hathaway Lee, in college. They were married almost four years when Mrs. Roosevelt gave birth to baby Alice. Two days later, Teddy's wife and mom died . . . on the same day. There was a double funeral, a new baby, and enough tears and grief to sink a ship. Roosevelt was in a state of shock. He gave baby Alice to his sister and went to his ranch in North Dakota. After a two-year hiatus from his life, he ran into Edith Carow, his childhood sweetheart, again in New York. They rekindled their relationship and eventually married. These two would have five kids together. During their marriage, Roosevelt served as a police commissioner, assistant secretary of the navy, and even governor of New York. In 1900, he was elected vice president for William McKinley. There were six Roosevelt children, and they would literally leave their mark on the Executive Mansion like no other first kids have done.

# ALICE LEE ROOSEVELT LONGWORTH

was born on February 12, 1884. Alice has earned a place in history as one of the most colorful and rowdy first kids ever. Being a president's daughter did not deter her from "living on the edge." Alice was spotted betting at the race track, gambling in card games, smoking, and drinking. Nothing and no one stopped her.

When she came into the White House at seventeen, she brought her collection of pets with her. Among her favorites were a green snake named Emily Spinach and a Pekinese that danced on its hind legs. Wild child Alice earned the nickname Princess Alice among Washington elite society. She refused to go to school outside her home when her family moved into the Executive Mansion.

In 1905, the president sent Alice on a goodwill trip to the Far East along with other officials and congressmen. Alice Roosevelt married a congressman from that trip, Nicholas Longworth, in the most famous White House wedding of all time on February 17, 1906. The event took place in the East Room and more than seven hundred people attended. Gifts piled in from all around the globe and reporters covered the event for weeks after it was over. Alice remained married to Longworth until his death in 1931. She lived to be ninety-six and died on February 20, 1980.

Alice Roosevelt at age eighteen (1902).

# THEODORE "TED" ROOSEVELT JR.

was born on September 13, 1887. Ted Jr. got to see the White House on visits home but mainly lived at his boarding school (Groton Preparatory) in Massachusetts. Eventually college-bound, Ted wanted to go to West Point, but Harvard won out because it was his father's alma mater. Ted Jr., inspired by his father, served in World War I. He married Eleanor Butler Alexander in 1910 and they had

Ted Jr. with a pet parrot (1902).

four children. Ted was appointed assistant secretary of the navy by President Warren Harding. Over his lifetime, Ted served as governor general of the Philippine Islands and the governor of Puerto Rico. He also attained the rank of brigadier general in World War II. Ted Jr. died during World War II on July 12, 1944. Some historians report that his death was due to a heart attack. He was fifty-six.

# KERMIT ROOSEVELT

Kermit riding a horse (1907).

was born on October 10, 1889, in Oyster Bay, New York. Kermit was twelve years old when his dad became president. He lived in the White House only during holiday times due to boarding school. Kermit was a hunter and went on many outings with his dad, who enjoyed the same interests. He really wanted to be a soldier. Before the United States joined the World War I efforts, Kermit was so determined that he enlisted in the British army, as a captain. When America entered the war efforts three years later, Kermit transferred to the American forces. Kermit eventually married Belle Wyatt Willard and had four children. He later joined British forces again in World War II as a major. He died of a self-inflicted gunshot wound on June 4, 1943. History relates that Kermit's mom, Edith Roosevelt, was never told of his suicide, only that he died of heart failure. Kermit was fifty-three when he died.

## ETHEL CAROW ROOSEVELT DERBY

was born on August 13, 1891. Ethel was ten years old when her dad became president. It was a tradition when the girls completed grammar or finishing school that a formal reception celebrating the occasion be held. Ethel's debut party was held in the White House. There were large orchestras, dancing, and more than four hundred guests in attendance. Ethel invited her good friend Helen Taft to the event.

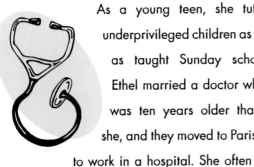

As a young teen, she tutored underprivileged children as well as taught Sunday school. Ethel married a doctor who was ten years older than she, and they moved to Paris to work in a hospital. She often drove ambulances. Ethel and her husband had four children. She died at the age of eighty-six on December 10, 1977.

Edith with her mother (1904).

## ARCHIBALD "ARCHIE" BULLOCH ROOSEVELT

was born on April 9, 1894. Archie was seven years old when his family exploded into the White House. Archie loved living in his new home and considered it his own personal playground. You could find Archie on a pair of stilts walking through the

Quentin and Archie play with a camera (1902).

hallway upstairs. Sometimes he would race his bike with his brother Quentin in that same hallway. Archie and Quentin along with their friends formed a posse called the White House Gang. The gang's job was to drop water balloons from the roof of the White House on the guards, scare visitors, annoy staff, and just about anything else

they could think of. Archie loved his pony, Algonquin. He often rode him to school and around the grounds of the White House. He eventually served with the U.S. army in World War I, where he was wounded severely, shattering his knee and arm, and in World War II where he was wounded once more. He was awarded Croix de Guerre by the French government, the Bronze Star, two Silver Stars, and a Purple Heart. Archie married Grace Lockwood and together they had four children. He worked on Wall Street. He died of a stroke on October 13, 1979.

# QUENTIN ROOSEVELT

was the baby of the Roosevelt family, arriving on November 19, 1897. Quentin was only three years old when his dad assumed the presidency. This little toddler struck fear in grown White House staffers and cabinet members. Quentin was a charter member of the White House Gang, which meant staging wars on the White House lawn with water guns and exploring all the crawl spaces within 1600 Pennsylvania Avenue. Quentin and his friend Charlie Taft were once caught launching spitballs at an official presidential portrait of Andrew Jackson. Quentin was fearless in childhood and also in adulthood. While he was a sophomore at Harvard, he enlisted in the army to fight in World War I. He was anxious to be a pilot, quickly completing the training to qualify for the American Air Corps, and went to France to assist in fighting the Germans. On July 14, 1918, German fighter planes shot down the youngest son of Theodore Roosevelt. Quentin died behind enemy lines at age twenty.

President Roosevelt with his four sons (1904).

The Roosevelt family (circa 1903).

# FAST FACTS

★ President Roosevelt's behavior was often as rowdy as his kids. Every day at four o'clock, he stopped working and the family had "children's hour." Sometimes he read to them, other times he told tales of his travels and hunts, and the hour almost always ended with rambunctious wrestling or a huge pillow fight.

★ Teddy Roosevelt and his wife pushed for a huge renovation and restoration of the White House that added the West Wing for offices and rebuilt the East Wing. The project cost almost $500,000.

★ Alice often carried her pet snake, Emily Spinach, in her purse. It made her friends very nervous.

★ Ethel and her brothers loved pets. The Roosevelts owned horses, a pony, dogs, birds, raccoons, guinea pigs, cats, snakes, frogs, a bear cub, mice, lizards, rats, and more!

★ White House events were many. Alice once decided to make a particular event more memorable. She pulled out a cap gun and started shooting.

TEDDY

★ Alice decided she was going to cut her own wedding cake. The knife that was handed to her to use was very dull. In typical Alice fashion, she quickly grabbed a sword from an army officer standing close by and used it to cut the cake.

★ Ted Jr.'s favorite pet was a macaw named Eli Yale.

★ Ted Jr. served as an usher at his sister Alice's wedding. There were also famous military leaders serving as ushers like Douglas McArthur and Ulysses Grant III.

★ Kermit had a pet kangaroo rat that he used to carry around in his coat pocket. He liked to feed it lumps of sugar from the breakfast table.

★ Kermit was an author. One of his published writings was a tribute to his brother Quentin who was killed in World War I, *Quentin Roosevelt: A Sketch with Letters.*

★ Ethel actually made the official seconding speech for Richard M. Nixon's nomination at the 1960 Republican National Convention.

# Presidential Hobbies

**BASEBALL**
George W. Bush

**BILLIARDS**
John Quincy Adams
James Garfield
Chester Arthur

**BOATING**
George H. W. Bush

**BOWLING**
Richard Nixon

**BOXING**
Theodore Roosevelt

**BRIDGE**
Dwight D. Eisenhower

**CANOEING**
Jimmy Carter

**CROQUET**
Rutherford B. Hayes

**DRIVING**
Rutherford B. Hayes

**FISHING**
George Washington
Thomas Jefferson
Grover Cleveland
Calvin Coolidge
Dwight D. Eisenhower
Lyndon Johnson
Jimmy Carter
George H. W. Bush

**FOOTBALL**
John F. Kennedy
Bill Clinton

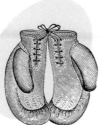

**GOLF**
William Taft
Woodrow Wilson
Warren Harding
Calvin Coolidge
Dwight D. Eisenhower
Richard Nixon
Gerald Ford
George H. W. Bush
Bill Clinton

**HORSEBACK RIDING**
George Washington
Thomas Jefferson
Andrew Jackson
Martin Van Buren
Zachary Taylor
William McKinley
Theodore Roosevelt
William Taft
Woodrow Wilson
Warren Harding
Lyndon Johnson
Ronald Reagan

**HORSESHOES**
George H. W. Bush

**HORTICULTURE**
Thomas Jefferson

**HUNTING**
Benjamin Harrison
Theodore Roosevelt
Lyndon Johnson

**JOGGING**
Gerald Ford
Jimmy Carter
George H. W. Bush
Bill Clinton

## JUDO
Theodore Roosevelt

## MECHANICAL HORSE
Calvin Coolidge

## MEDICINE BALL
Herbert Hoover

## PAINTING
Dwight D. Eisenhower

## PIANO
Harry Truman
Richard Nixon

## PITCHING HAY
Calvin Coolidge

## RUNNING
George W. Bush

## SAILING
Franklin D. Roosevelt
John F. Kennedy
Gerald Ford

## SAXOPHONE
Bill Clinton

## SHOOTING
Rutherford B. Hayes
Theodore Roosevelt

## SKIING
Gerald Ford
Jimmy Carter

## SOFTBALL
Jimmy Carter

## STAMP COLLECTING
Franklin D. Roosevelt

## SWIMMING
John Quincy Adams
Ulysses S. Grant
William McKinley
Woodrow Wilson
Franklin D. Roosevelt
Harry Truman
John F. Kennedy
Gerald Ford
Jimmy Carter
Ronald Reagan

## TENNIS
Theodore Roosevelt
Jimmy Carter
George H.W. Bush

## TRAPSHOOTING
Calvin Coolidge

## VIOLIN
Thomas Jefferson

## WALKING
Thomas Jefferson
John Quincy Adams
Abraham Lincoln
William McKinley
Woodrow Wilson

## WRESTLING
Abraham Lincoln
Theodore Roosevelt
Harry Truman

# The Tafts

President Taft with his wife, Helen, and their three children (1909).

## William H. Taft (1909-1913)

William Howard Taft was one of the few presidents who never really wanted the job. His goal in life was to be a Supreme Court justice. His wife, Nellie Taft, whose lifelong goal was to be the first lady, pressured this more than three-hundred-pound man into the job. Though she had a stroke two months after the inauguration, she recovered enough to be in command and host many memorable events as first lady. Despite his weight, President Taft was very physically active. His interests included golfing and baseball. He even started the tradition of the president throwing out the first pitch at baseball games. William Howard Taft also raised an eleven-year-old and a teenager in the White House.

# ROBERT ALPHONSO TAFT

was born on September 8, 1889. Robert was nineteen and a junior at Yale when his dad became president. He started in politics in the Ohio State House of Representatives. Later he ran for the U.S. Senate and won. His conservative beliefs and academic personality earned him the nickname

President Taft with his sons (1909).

Mr. Republican. He ran for the Republican presidential nomination three times but never won. Robert was successful in his own right serving as a senator who was popular with his constituents and fellow congressmen. Senator John F. Kennedy featured Robert Taft in his bestselling, Pulitzer Prize–winning book, *Profiles in Courage*. Robert died of cancer on July 31, 1953.

# HELEN HERRON TAFT MANNING

was born on August 1, 1891. Helen was seventeen and a freshman at Bryn Mawr College when her dad became the commander in chief. During childhood, Helen was educated in the Philippines while her dad was the appointed governor of the islands. In her second year at college, she took a brief leave of absence. She stepped in as first lady until her mom had recovered from a stroke. Helen later returned to Bryn Mawr and graduated magna cum laude. Only two years later,

Helen Taft (1911).

she became the school's dean. She later married a professor from Yale University named Fredrick Manning. They had two children together. Helen spent most of her life in higher education but also in dealing with women's suffrage and women's rights. She would be instrumental in getting the 19th Amendment passed, allowing women to vote for the first time. Helen Herron Taft Manning would live to be ninety-five years old. She died of complications from pneumonia on February 21, 1987.

# CHARLES "CHARLIE" PHELPS TAFT

was born on September 20, 1897. Charlie loved to play, and let's just say school was not a priority of his. These characteristics eventually got him access to the White House Gang and the title of "best friend" of Quentin Roosevelt while Taft was President Roosevelt's secretary of war. Once Charlie took over the White House switchboard while the staff was on their lunch break. He posed as a

Charlie Taft on vacation with his parents at Middle Bass Island (1908).

White House switchboard operator and chatted with callers who had phoned in. This first kid went to Yale. Charlie was very outgoing and popular. He was on the basketball and football teams, and president of the debating club. Charlie served in World War I as a first lieutenant of field artillery in the U.S. Army in France. After the war, he finished law school and went into business with his older brother, Robert. He married Eleanor Kellogg Chase and they had seven children together. He died June 24, 1983, at the age of eighty-five.

# FAST FACTS

★ First dad and president William Howard Taft served as a chief justice of the Supreme Court after having left the office of president. He is the only president in history to have done so.

☆ William Howard Taft once got stuck in a White House bathtub.

★ Mrs. Taft had all the cherry trees planted that are seen year after year blooming along the Potomac River. She used to live in Japan and they were a favorite of hers.

☆ The Tafts had four cars while in the White House.

★ The Tafts had a cow grazing on the White House lawn. It kept the grass from looking overgrown and provided fresh milk daily.

☆ The cow, named Pauline Wayne, lived in the garages with the automobiles. The garages had been converted from horse stables to house the new autos. The cow was one of the last "working" animals to live on the White House grounds.

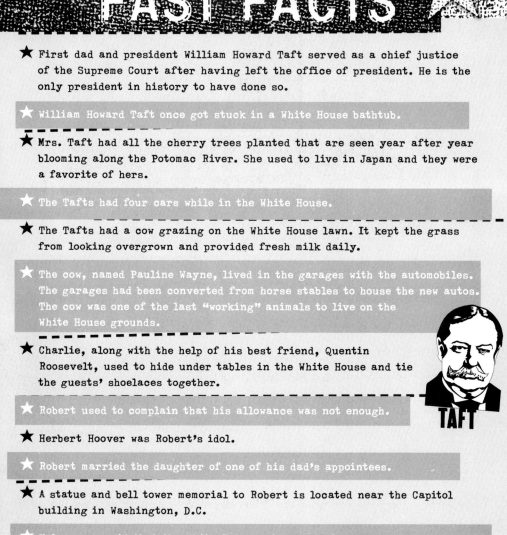

TAFT

★ Charlie, along with the help of his best friend, Quentin Roosevelt, used to hide under tables in the White House and tie the guests' shoelaces together.

☆ Robert used to complain that his allowance was not enough.

★ Herbert Hoover was Robert's idol.

☆ Robert married the daughter of one of his dad's appointees.

★ A statue and bell tower memorial to Robert is located near the Capitol building in Washington, D.C.

☆ Helen once said that the White House gates were always opened when her dad was president. People could drive or stroll through the grounds.

★ Helen made her debut after graduation with 1,200 guests in attendance to celebrate at the White House.

☆ Charlie was named after his wealthy uncle (his dad's brother).

*"Don't mind what he [the president] says. Upstairs here, he is just like any one of us, and we pay no attention to him."*
— *First Lady Edith Wilson*

# The Wilsons

*Woodrow Wilson (1913-1921)*

Woodrow Wilson was the 28th president of the United States. Not only did he bring new policies and beliefs to Washington with him, but he also brought three lovely daughters. The press could not get enough of them. The Wilson family was close and spent lots of time together in the White House. At night, they would sometimes gather around their father, upstairs in the Oval Room, and listen to him read aloud from some of his favorite novels. The White House staff of the Wilson administration reported that President Wilson was a big ham and told jokes, performed, and danced with his wife and daughters. The Wilson family's joy was shattered by the death of First Lady Ellen Wilson. For months, President Wilson wore a black armband each day. After sixteen months, he married Edith Galt and she became his new first lady and eventual right arm when he had a stroke before the end of his term. Edith would attend meetings, sign important papers, receive guests, and, in general, help run the country for the last months of his presidency.

# MARGARET WOODROW WILSON

Margaret Wilson (circa 1910).

was born on April 16, 1886. Margaret was twenty-six years old when her dad became president. Margaret and her sisters would often don disguises and hit the streets of Washington, D.C. They would pretend to be clueless tourists and do things like wait in long lines to buy tickets for public tours of the nation's capital. Margaret's dream was to be a singer. It came true when she teamed with the Red Cross and traveled the country and abroad performing for soldiers during World War I. When Margaret's mom, Ellen, died, Margaret stepped in and acted as first lady until her dad remarried. She worked for various social causes and in advertising after leaving the White House. When her dad died, he left most of his estate to his new wife, Edith. However, Margaret did receive $2,500 per year with one stipulation: that she never get married—she never did. Margaret began studying religions of India and eventually moved to Pondicherry, India. She never returned to the United States and died at the age of fifty-seven on February 12, 1944.

# JESSIE WOODROW WILSON SAYRE

was born on August 28, 1887. She was a gifted student who did very well in school. Jessie married Francis Sayre, a Harvard law professor, and they had three children together. After graduation, Jessie focused on some of the important political issues of the day. The biggest injustice in her opinion was the rights of women. She led marches and organized protests every chance she got. Jessie was the one who convinced her famous father to support the 19th Amendment allowing women to vote for the first time. She also fought for America to join the League of Nations and was even encouraged to run for the U.S. Senate. At the height of her popularity, Jessie died after complications from surgery on January 15, 1933. She lived to be forty-five years old.

Jessie Wilson (circa 1910).

# ELEANOR "NELLIE" RANDOLPH WILSON MCADOO

was born on October 16, 1889. Nellie had just graduated from Princeton when her dad became president. She was immediately thrust into the national spotlight. Nellie loved all the attention, but she especially loved her dad's secretary of the treasury, William McAdoo. It seemed like they were almost inseparable. The only problem with these two

Nellie Wilson (circa 1910).

lovebirds was the fact that Nellie was twenty-three and William was a fifty-year-old widowed grandfather who had six children of his own. After two proposals, they finally married in a small Blue Room ceremony in the White House. They had two children but divorced after more than twenty years of marriage. Nellie wrote short stories and several books and became a sought-after speaker and commentator. She died April 5, 1967, at the ripe old age of seventy-seven.

# FAST FACTS

★ Due to the fact that most men were serving in World War I, President Wilson used sheep instead of gardeners at the White House. They kept the grass neat and trimmed and Wilson would shear them and donate the proceeds from the wool to the Red Cross. More than $50,000 was earned from the wool. The Wilsons at one point had a flock of 18 sheep, including a ram named Old Ike.

★ President Wilson spent his first night as president alone with his family. He did not have an inaugural ball.

★ Woodrow Wilson was very protective of his first daughters even though they were twenty-three, twenty-five, and twenty-six when they moved into the White House.

★ The Wilson family left their mark on the White House by renovating part of the attic to include a painting room and guest rooms.

★ Margaret's bedroom in the White House was the same room in which Abraham Lincoln signed the Emancipation Proclamation.

★ When President Wilson left office, he was very ill. Margaret lived in New York and would visit him each weekend.

**WILSON**

★ During her early adult life, Margaret worked to improve child welfare laws.

★ Margaret suffered a nervous breakdown due to all the things she had witnessed while trying to comfort the servicemen.

★ Jessie's wedding ceremony was half Episcopalian and half Presbyterian. The Wilsons were Presbyterian and the Sayres were Episcopalian.

★ The White House had been the backdrop for ten weddings and Jessie's would be the eleventh. The eleven weddings includes every wedding ever held there, not just first kid weddings.

★ Francis Sayre Jr. (Jessie's son) was born in the White House.

★ Nellie wrote a book about her family entitled *The Woodrow Wilsons*.

★ Nellie was instrumental in forming the Woodrow Wilson Foundation.

# The Hardings

*President Harding and his wife, Florence (1920).*

## Warren G. Harding (1921-1923)

Warren Harding was America's 29th president. Though his entire presidency was racked with gossip and scandal, his antics before becoming commander in chief were questionable as well. Harding was dubbed "ineffective" by most historians, but this was for good reason. Harding gambled away the White House china as well as having all the White House closets enlarged for his massive wardrobe. Harding's cabinet did not help his failing image, since they participated in the famous Teapot Dome scandal, in which the cabinet leased military oil reserves for personal gain. Almost a year before he was elected president, some gossip surfaced about Senator Harding's affair with a woman named Nan Britton, who gave birth to his child. This rumor did little to harm Harding's campaign for president because he did not respond to it. Harding was known to have sent child support payments to Ms. Britton through a broker, though he never saw or spoke to his child. Elizabeth Ann Blessing lived her entire life out of the spotlight that most first kids experience. President Harding died while in office on August 2, 1923.

# How Many First Kids Were Born This Month?

JANUARY — 6

FEBRUARY — 10

MARCH — 13

APRIL — 16

MAY — 10

JUNE — 3

JULY — 19

AUGUST — 19

SEPTEMBER — 15

OCTOBER — 14

NOVEMBER — 8

DECEMBER — 12

UNKNOWN — 6

President Coolidge with his wife, Grace, and two sons (circa 1920).

"When he went, the power and the glory of the presidency went with him."
— Calvin Coolidge, on the death of his son Cal Jr.

# The Coolidges

## Calvin Coolidge (1923-1929)

The Coolidges inherited the White House from Warren Harding, who died midway through his term. Calvin Coolidge would not only complete Harding's term, but would also be elected to one of his own. This stoic governor of Massachusetts, who was born in Vermont, served his country well and presided over the Roaring Twenties when the economy soared to new heights. He did not have much of a public persona, but he got the job done. Coolidge brought two athletic boys with him to Washington, but left with only one.

## JOHN COOLIDGE

was born September 7, 1906. John was at Amherst College while his father was president. He was a boxer, actor, and a singer. President Coolidge had some unusual requirements of his children. One of those involved dress code. When his children ate at the table in the White House, they were required to wear a suit

John Coolidge (1923).

John and Cal Jr. playing the violin and a banjo (1920).

and tie! John never liked the fact that Secret Service men would accompany him on every date during his college years. One college sweetheart, Florence Trumbull, didn't seem to mind and married John in 1929. Florence was no stranger to politics. Her father was the governor of Connecticut. They had one child together. He became a traveling passenger agent for the Hartford, New York, and New Haven Railroads in multiple cities, and in 1938 served as a delegate to the Republican National Convention. In retirement, John began purchasing buildings in Vermont for preservation. These buildings are now a campus of sorts, housing the Calvin Coolidge State Historic Site, in Plymouth Notch, Vermont. John died May 31, 2000, at the age of ninety-three.

# CALVIN "CAL JR." COOLIDGE JR.

was born April 13, 1908. This first son was very talkative, a trait that he did not share with his presidential father. President Coolidge required his sons to work and learn the value of a dollar. Cal Jr. got a job one summer helping on a tobacco farm. Some of the other workers there were curious why the son of a president would work in such a place. Cal Jr.'s reply to the workers was simple: "If my father were your father, you would." Cal Jr. loved the White House for one reason . . . the tennis courts. He played tennis one day with just his tennis shoes and no socks. Cal developed a blister on his foot but ignored it thinking it was nothing important. This minor blister became infected and blood poisoning claimed Cal Jr.'s life on July 7, 1924, at the age of sixteen.

Calvin Coolidge Jr. (1923).

# FAST FACTS

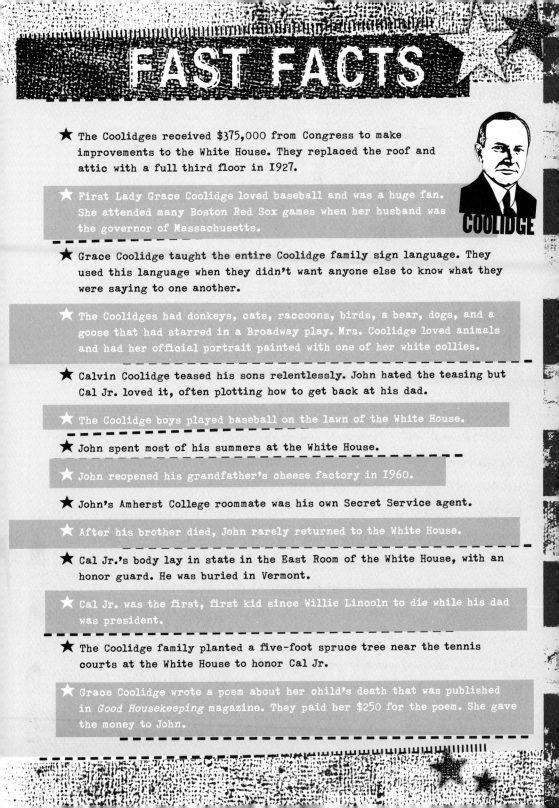

★ The Coolidges received $375,000 from Congress to make improvements to the White House. They replaced the roof and attic with a full third floor in 1927.

★ First Lady Grace Coolidge loved baseball and was a huge fan. She attended many Boston Red Sox games when her husband was the governor of Massachusetts.

**COOLIDGE**

★ Grace Coolidge taught the entire Coolidge family sign language. They used this language when they didn't want anyone else to know what they were saying to one another.

★ The Coolidges had donkeys, cats, raccoons, birds, a bear, dogs, and a goose that had starred in a Broadway play. Mrs. Coolidge loved animals and had her official portrait painted with one of her white collies.

★ Calvin Coolidge teased his sons relentlessly. John hated the teasing but Cal Jr. loved it, often plotting how to get back at his dad.

★ The Coolidge boys played baseball on the lawn of the White House.

★ John spent most of his summers at the White House.

★ John reopened his grandfather's cheese factory in 1960.

★ John's Amherst College roommate was his own Secret Service agent.

★ After his brother died, John rarely returned to the White House.

★ Cal Jr.'s body lay in state in the East Room of the White House, with an honor guard. He was buried in Vermont.

★ Cal Jr. was the first, first kid since Willie Lincoln to die while his dad was president.

★ The Coolidge family planted a five-foot spruce tree near the tennis courts at the White House to honor Cal Jr.

★ Grace Coolidge wrote a poem about her child's death that was published in *Good Housekeeping* magazine. They paid her $250 for the poem. She gave the money to John.

# The Hoovers

## Herbert Hoover
## (1929-1933)

erbert Hoover was elected our 31st president of the United States in 1928. He brought with him an amazing set of credentials. Hoover was a Stanford-educated engineer and became a multimillionaire from the mining industry. And last, but certainly not least, he was the secretary of commerce under not one, but two presidents. He came to the White House guaranteeing every American "a car in every garage and a chicken in every pot." Unfortunately, his promise never came to pass. The stock market crashed in 1929, which set off the Great Depression. Millions of Americans lost everything they owned. Hoover tried to help, but it was perceived that he didn't care because he was wealthy and out of touch. Throughout these hard times, there were three adults who stuck by him: his wife and his two grown sons.

## HERBERT CLARK HOOVER JR.

was born on August 8, 1903, in England. Herbert Jr. was highly intelligent and a straight "A" student, overcoming the fact that he was hearing-impaired and wore a hearing aid. His college experience included earning his bachelor's degree at Stanford and his master's degree at Harvard Business School. While his father was president, Herbert Jr. had tuberculosis and was recovering in North Carolina. After his recuperation, Herbert Jr. made his mark in geology, inventing many key devices that are still in use today to detect oil. His own political aspirations found him serving as the assistant secretary of state for President Eisenhower. Herbert Jr. married

Herbert Hoover Jr. in front of a plane in Atlanta, Georgia (1929).

Margaret Watson, and they had three children. He became quite wealthy through all his endeavors. He died in California on April 9, 1969, at the age of sixty-five.

# ALLAN HENRY HOOVER

was born on July 17, 1907. He didn't like the White House at all, saying that it gave him the willies. He graduated from Stanford and proceeded to Harvard Business School. After graduation, Allan took over management of his father's California ranch. He took advantage of a part of FDR's New Deal, where the government paid ranchers and farmers not to grow certain crops so that prices would be high. With this and other business tactics at different ranches across the state, Allan soon became a rich man. He was also a mining executive and investment banker. Allan and his wife, Margaret, had two children. He died on November 8, 1993, at the age of eighty-six.

Allan Hoover graduating from Stanford (1929).

# FAST FACTS

★ When President and Mrs. Hoover didn't want anyone to hear their conversations, they spoke Chinese to each other.

★ The Hoovers purchased a private mountain retreat to get away from Washington. The retreat was called Camp Rapidan and was located in Virginia.

★ First Lady Lou Hoover often held Girl Scout retreats at Camp Rapidan. She helped train adults to mentor girls and teach camping and exploring skills.

★ When Lou Hoover died, there were more than 200 Girl Scouts at her funeral.

★ At nine years of age, President Herbert Hoover became an orphan.

★ Herbert Jr. helped develop technology for weapons that helped the American armed services during World War II.

★ Herbert Jr. was twenty-five when his dad became president and Allan was twenty-one.

**HOOVER**

★ Herbert Jr. was portrayed as a "genius" in *Time* magazine for his contributions as an engineer to U.S. weapon systems that helped America in World War II.

★ Allan had two pet alligators that lived in the White House.

★ Allan once hosted a Christmas party in the White House for 250 guests. Jazz music filled the dance floor, and they dined in the State Dining Room. It was the only time President Hoover allowed dancing at the White House.

★ Allan was twenty-one when he became a first kid.

★ Allan and his wife moved to Greenwich, Connecticut, where they helped run many organizations and foundations affiliated with his famous father.

"Sometimes the best way to keep peace in the family is to keep the members of the family apart for a while."
— Franklin D. Roosevelt

President Roosevelt with his wife, Eleanor, and five children (1915).

# The Franklin D. Roosevelts

## Franklin D. Roosevelt (1933-1945)

Franklin D. Roosevelt served as the 32nd president of the United States of America. The amazing thing about his administration is that it would go on for more than twelve years . . . he was elected four times. Things have changed today—presidents can only serve two terms, for a total of eight years. He entered office with a disability that he never allowed to define him or his leadership. He had polio and was diagnosed with it when he was thirty-nine years old. FDR lived with the disease for eleven years before he was elected president. He used a wheelchair, which he actually made himself, but he never allowed anyone to photograph him in it. He wanted to maintain an appearance of "strength" to America. FDR and his wife, Eleanor, were the very definition of strength. They made a phenomenal difference in America by helping the nation survive during the biggest financial depression in history.

FDR with Sara (his mother), Eleanor, Elliot, Franklin Jr., John, Anna, James, and their German Shepherd (1919).

# ANNA ELEANOR ROOSEVELT DALL BOETTIGER HALSTED

was born on May 3, 1906. Once Eleanor designed a wire cage of sorts especially for young Anna. Mrs. Roosevelt would hang the cage outside the window of her home . . . with Anna in it! She said it was for the purpose of providing Anna with plenty of fresh air. Anna actually survived her childhood and went to college at Cornell. There she studied agriculture. Soon she fell in love and married Curtis Dall, who was ten years older than her. After six years and two kids, Anna divorced him and moved back to the White House with her kids. Two years later, Anna married again, this time to John Boettiger, a successful reporter for the *Chicago Tribune.* They moved to Seattle, then Phoenix, where the couple began their own newspaper venture. In 1945, Anna's dad died. In 1949, the marriage ended and so did the newspaper. She eventually married Dr. James A. Halsted and settled in California. Anna and her husband traveled the world and she lived to be sixty-nine years old. Anna died of throat cancer on December 1, 1975.

# JAMES "JIMMY" ROOSEVELT

was born December 23, 1907. Jimmy was twenty-six when his dad became president. He would have several different jobs and occupations during his lifetime, such as: insurance agent, president of a corporation, military aide and White House secretary for his father, marine captain, author, war hero, politician, congressman for California (five terms), movie producer, campaign worker, committee member for social security and Medicare benefits, and United Nations delegate. The FDR Presidential Library records that Jimmy was married four times and fathered seven children. Jimmy had been diagnosed with Parkinson's disease and had many health problems as a result of a stroke. He died at the age of eighty-three on August 13, 1991.

## FRANKLIN ROOSEVELT

was born on March 18, 1909. He died on November 8, 1909, due to complications from the flu.

## ELLIOTT ROOSEVELT

was born on September 23, 1910. He purposely failed the entrance exam to Harvard University, shocking the educational traditions of the Roosevelt family. The public was always critical and judgmental, claiming that Elliot received this or that because his dad was the president. Elliott served bravely in the war as an amazing and daring pilot, but his business practices were said to have been scandalous. Though not even a college graduate, he authored nine books. Elliot was married five times and had nine children. He died of heart failure on October 27, 1990. He was eighty years old.

## FRANKLIN DELANO ROOSEVELT JR.

Franklin Jr. with his parents (1935).

was born on August 17, 1914. Franklin Jr. was eighteen when his father was elected president, and he celebrated graduating from Groton Prep School by traveling to Europe. He attended Harvard and went on to serve with honor in the U.S. Navy, winning both the Purple Heart and the Silver Star. President Harry S Truman appointed Franklin Jr. to the U.S. Civil Rights Commission. President Kennedy appointed him undersecretary of commerce, and President Lyndon B.

Johnson appointed him to the Equal Opportunity Commission. Franklin was married five times, fathering five children. He died on his seventy-fourth birthday, August 17, 1988.

# JOHN ASPINWALL ROOSEVELT

was born on March 13, 1916. He was considered the mildest of the Roosevelt children. He was only sixteen when he became a first kid. Though he graduated from Groton Prep and Harvard University, John would not follow his first dad or his first brothers into politics. Instead, he settled for being a department store clerk for years, until he enlisted in the U.S. Navy. John married a girl from Boston, Anne Lindsay Clark. This marriage would last twenty-seven years before they divorced. John remarried only once, to Irene McAlpin. He served with distinction in the war, earning a Bronze Star. According to his family and the press, the only questionable or controversial thing he ever really did was become a Republican and campaign for Eisenhower, Nixon, and Ronald Reagan. This was a shock to his Democratic bloodline. He had five children and died of a heart attack on April 27, 1981. He was sixty-eight years old.

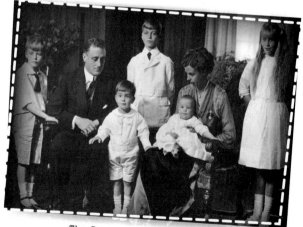

The Roosevelt family (1919).

# FAST FACTS

★ President Franklin Delano Roosevelt and his wife, Eleanor, were fifth cousins.

★ Franklin Delano Roosevelt had a little black Scottish terrier, Fala.

★ The Roosevelt family loved to eat scrambled eggs together. Both Franklin Delano Roosevelt and Eleanor were known to whip them up in the White House kitchen for their visiting family.

★ Franklin Delano Roosevelt stopped the tradition of the Easter Egg Roll at the White House. (It returned in 1953.)

★ Among all of Franklin Delano Roosevelt and Eleanor's children, they had 19 marriages.

★ The Roosevelts always celebrated Christmas together at the White House while Franklin Delano Roosevelt was in office. Eleanor purchased gifts not only for her own kids and grandkids but also for everyone who served in any way at the White House. This included police, Secret Service, gardeners, cooks, servants, valets, doormen, etc.

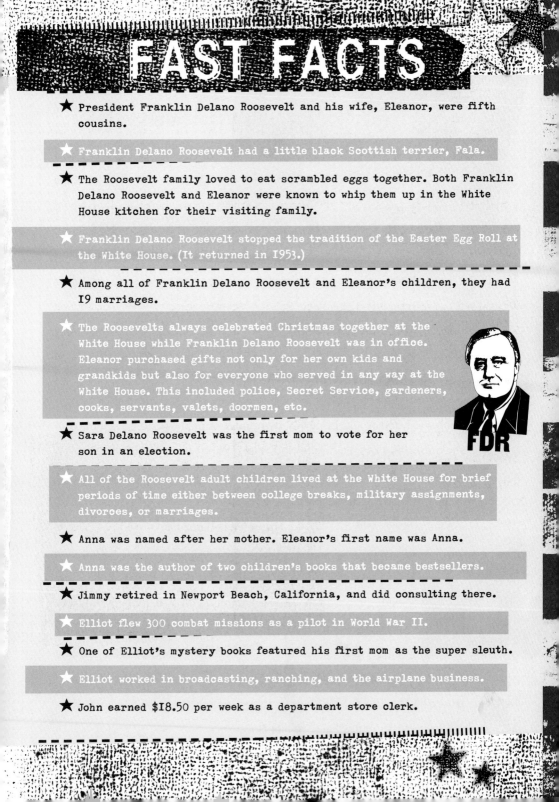

FDR

★ Sara Delano Roosevelt was the first mom to vote for her son in an election.

★ All of the Roosevelt adult children lived at the White House for brief periods of time either between college breaks, military assignments, divorces, or marriages.

★ Anna was named after her mother. Eleanor's first name was Anna.

★ Anna was the author of two children's books that became bestsellers.

★ Jimmy retired in Newport Beach, California, and did consulting there.

★ Elliot flew 300 combat missions as a pilot in World War II.

★ One of Elliot's mystery books featured his first mom as the super sleuth.

★ Elliot worked in broadcasting, ranching, and the airplane business.

★ John earned $18.50 per week as a department store clerk.

"I remember crying myself to sleep on my first night in the place. It all looked so shabby." — Margaret Truman...on the aging, sagging White House

# The Trumans

## Harry S Truman (1945-1953)

President Truman with his wife, Bess, and daughter, Margaret (1950).

arry S Truman entered the White House as vice president, taking over for beloved president Franklin D. Roosevelt, who had just passed away. Truman was now president number 33 and would bring his own brand of politics and parenting with him. When he arrived in 1945, the White House was falling apart. The Trumans moved but noticed cracks in all the walls as well as sagging floors. They eventually moved out and into Blair House, which was normally used for state guests. The Trumans lived there from 1948 to 1952. Congress immediately approved funds for a full restoration of the White House. The Executive Mansion was completely gutted down to the outside walls. A famous addition during renovation was the Truman balcony. In fact, the Treasury Department had to engrave a new back for the twenty-dollar bill because the picture on the White House had changed due to the renovations. The Trumans did get to finally move back to the White House on March 27, 1952. In fact, Harry Truman would lead the nation on the very first televised tour of the "new" White House.

# MARGARET TRUMAN DANIEL

Margaret Truman (1945).

was born on February 17, 1924, in Independence, Missouri. When she was just ten years old, her father was elected to the U.S. Senate. Because the Senate is located in Washington, D.C., Margaret would go to school half the year in Missouri (public school) and half the year in Washington (private girls' school). It was tough to make friends and fit in. Margaret was an only child and didn't have siblings to rely on for friendship. Margaret was twenty-one when her dad assumed the presidency. She was a college student at George Washington University. Margaret was already a pro at political life in Washington because of her days as a senator's and vice president's kid. Her dream was to be a professional singer, and she did take lessons from famous teachers, toured the country, and even signed a record deal. Margaret sang professionally for a time and later made her way into radio and television. She married a respected reporter, named Clifford Daniel, three years after her first parents left the White House. She first wrote a memoir on herself and then

Margaret takes her Irish setter puppy for a walk at the White House (1945).

a book about White House pets. Margaret Truman is now hailed for the bestseller on her famous dad, *Harry S Truman*, and her mom, *Bess W. Truman*. So far, Margaret Truman has written a total of twenty-six books and has edited two more. Her mysteries are bestselling political thrillers. Margaret and Clifford had four sons together. She died on January 29, 2008, at eighty-three years old.

# FAST FACTS

★ Harry Truman once threatened to punch a reporter in the nose after a harsh newspaper criticism of his daughter Margaret's singing.

★ Truman redesigned the official presidential seal.

★ Mrs. Truman was an avid sports fan. She loved baseball.

★ When Margaret was eight years old, her mom and dad bought her a Steinway piano for Christmas.

★ Margaret was named after her dad's sister Mary. Her real name was Mary Margaret Truman.

★ Margaret was a natural entertainer. She loved to dress up and use old clothes and shoes from the family attic.

★ Margaret once convinced a friend to hoist her up so that she could touch the chandelier that hung in the State Dinning Room. She grabbed on to it in order to get her balance, and he left her there hanging and screaming. White House staff had to help her down.

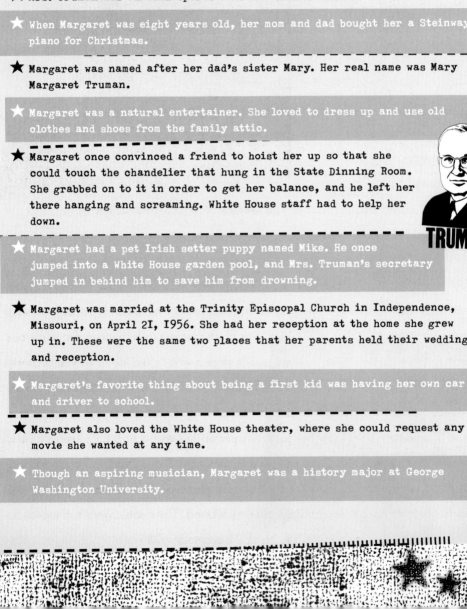

TRUMAN

★ Margaret had a pet Irish setter puppy named Mike. He once jumped into a White House garden pool, and Mrs. Truman's secretary jumped in behind him to save him from drowning.

★ Margaret was married at the Trinity Episcopal Church in Independence, Missouri, on April 21, 1956. She had her reception at the home she grew up in. These were the same two places that her parents held their wedding and reception.

★ Margaret's favorite thing about being a first kid was having her own car and driver to school.

★ Margaret also loved the White House theater, where she could request any movie she wanted at any time.

★ Though an aspiring musician, Margaret was a history major at George Washington University.

# The Eisenhowers

## Dwight D. Eisenhower
## (1953-1961)

Dwight D. Eisenhower was the 34th president of the United States. He was incredibly popular as well as an accomplished and decorated war hero who many today credit for winning World War II. People remembered this during his run for the White House in 1952. Eisenhower's slogan was "I like Ike!" His wife, Mamie, was an adored first lady at the White House. He would move into the White House and stay there for eight years. Eisenhower loved golf, but the White House putting green had become the local hangout for squirrels in Washington, D.C. The president got so ticked because of this that he enlisted the Secret Service's help. They developed Operation Exodus to get rid of the squirrels. The plan was successful and the president got to work on his putting game anytime he wished. The Eisenhowers had two kids, although only one would live to see his dad become president.

# DOUD "ICKY" DWIGHT EISENHOWER

was born on September 24, 1917. Unfortunately he would not live to celebrate his fourth birthday and died of scarlet fever on January 2, 1921. He is buried today on the Dwight D. Eisenhower Library grounds in Abilene, Kansas.

# JOHN SHELDON DOUD EISENHOWER

was born on August 3, 1922. John grew up on military bases all over the world. This first kid was twenty-nine years old when his father became president and was already married to Barbara Jean Thompson. John did have a great educational resume, having gone to West Point and Columbia University. He had many careers, including Korean War hero, White House aide, U.S ambassador to Belgium for Nixon, and book author. Presidential DNA would elude John, but not his son Dwight (known as David, his middle name). David married Julie Nixon, the daughter of Richard Nixon, John's dad's vice president. John had four kids, but his marriage would end in divorce in 1986. He married Joanne Thompson in 1988. He currently lives in Trappe, Maryland.

John Eisenhower (1945).

The Eisenhowers on Christmas day, 1957. From left to right: David, Mamie, Barbara, Mary, John, Anne, Dwight, and Susan.

# FAST FACTS

★ Dwight Eisenhower was the first chief executive of all fifty states.

★ Ike was the first president to have a hole-in-one in a golf game.

★ President Eisenhower loved to barbecue.

★ President Eisenhower had a piano added to the presidential plane to make his wife, First Lady Mamie Eisenhower, forget her fear of flying.

★ Helicopters began transporting President Eisenhower from place to place during his administration.

★ John earned a master of arts in English at Columbia University.

★ John's rank in the army was brigadier general before retiring in 1974 (U.S. Army Reserves).

★ John's youngest daughter, Mary Jean Eisenhower, was christened in the Blue Room of the White House in 1956.

★ David Eisenhower (John's son) was in the White House a lot as a young first grandson. He put notes behind all the pictures in the White House when his grandfather's administration was over. The notes said, "I will return!"

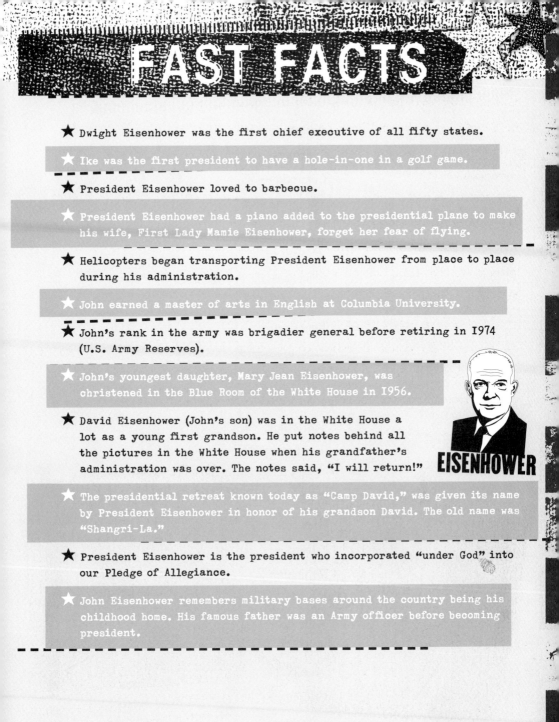

EISENHOWER

★ The presidential retreat known today as "Camp David," was given its name by President Eisenhower in honor of his grandson David. The old name was "Shangri-La."

★ President Eisenhower is the president who incorporated "under God" into our Pledge of Allegiance.

★ John Eisenhower remembers military bases around the country being his childhood home. His famous father was an Army officer before becoming president.

# Birthplaces of First Kids

Arkansas — 1

California — 6

Colorado — 1

Connecticut — 4

Georgia — 3

Hawaii — 1

Illinois — 6

Indiana — 7

Kentucky — 5

Massachusetts — 11

Missouri — 3

New Hampshire — 3

New Jersey — 2

New York — 20

Ohio — 23

Pennsylvania — 1

Tennessee — 7

Texas — 7

Virginia — 25

Washington, D.C. — 15

Canada — 1

England — 2

France — 1

Germany — 1

Russia — 1

"If you bungle raising your children, I don't think whatever else you do well, matters very much."
— Jackie Kennedy

# The Kennedys

John F. Kennedy (1961-1963)

President Kennedy with his wife, Jackie, and two children (1963).

John F. Kennedy is a legendary president. Possibly because his young life came to an abrupt end after only 1,000 days in office. Whatever the reason, America was, and still is, fascinated with the Kennedys. They had two very young children when they entered the White House. Mrs. Kennedy would adopt the White House as her very own home by updating it, restoring it, and redecorating it. President Kennedy would make monumental decisions within its walls that would change the nation forever. The Kennedys were like royalty and treated as American movie stars. Because of this intriguing and warm young family, the White House, for the first time, in a long time, seemed like a family home rather than a symbol of the American government.

## CAROLINE BOUVIER KENNEDY SCHLOSSBERG

was born on November 27, 1957. Mrs. Kennedy had selected children of her friends and staff members to attend school at the White House. The classroom was located on the third floor in the White House solarium. There were eleven students, including Caroline. Mrs. Kennedy started the school when Caroline was in kindergarten. Many days during school, Caroline would eat lunch with her mom or enjoy a visit from her dad. Caroline's favorite pet was her pony given to her by Vice President Lyndon B. Johnson.

Her pony's name was Macaroni, and he received mail from children all over the nation at the White House. Caroline's mom used to let Macaroni pull them in a sleigh around the snowy White House grounds in the winter. Caroline's favorite activities as a child were reading, playing with her brother, and her dolls. Caroline's mom remarried in 1968 and Caroline often traveled around the world with her mom and her new husband, Aristotle Onassis. She earned a degree in fine arts from Radcliffe College and also graduated from Columbia Law School.

She married Edwin Schlossberg in 1986, and they have three children together. She still loves to read and enjoys poetry. She also still loves dolls. As a matter of fact, the John F. Kennedy Library and Museum held a special exhibit entitled Caroline Kennedy's Doll Collection (1961–1963). These dolls were all given to her when her dad was in the White House. They came from thirty different countries and were gifts from world leaders. There are seventy-seven dolls in total. Currently, Carolyn lives in New York City and serves as president of the John F. Kennedy Library Foundation. She has championed multimillion-dollar fund-raising efforts for New York City's public schools and continues to be involved. She is the only living member of President Kennedy's immediate family.

Caroline Kennedy jumping on a trampoline (1963).

Caroline and John Jr. having a picnic on the South Lawn of the White House (1963).

# JOHN FITZGERALD KENNEDY JR.

was born on November 25, 1960. He made his way into the Kennedy family only weeks after the election. His love of flying began with watching the helicopters land in his front yard at the White House. He enjoyed playing with his dogs, Pushinka and Charlie. He was famous for wandering into his dad's office and dancing or hiding under the desk. He loved to get candy out of the candy jar of Mrs. Lincoln, JFK's secretary. He is probably most famous to Americans as the three-year-old who

John Kennedy Jr. playing under his father's desk in the Oval Office (1963).

saluted his deceased father's casket as it passed by him in the funeral procession.

John was a daring and risk-taking child, teenager, and adult. He paraglided, kayaked, roller bladed, and loved anything involved with speed. Unlike all the other Kennedy men, John chose to attend Brown University, instead of Harvard, and New York University Law School. John became a lawyer and an assistant district attorney. He was the editor in chief and founder of *George* magazine. John dated a lot of famous women, much to the delight of the press, but finally settled down, marrying Carolyn Bessette in 1996. John loved to fly and eventually purchased his own plane. Tragically, when things were at their brightest, John died in a plane crash off Martha's Vineyard along with his wife, Carolyn, on July 16, 1999, at the age of thirty-eight.

# PATRICK BOUVIER KENNEDY

was born August 7, 1963. Unfortunately, Patrick was premature and suffered from complications. He died on August 9, 1963.

# FAST FACTS

★ First Lady Jacqueline Kennedy had a wonderful playground built for her children at the White House. It was complete with swing set, playhouse, trampoline, a slide, a teeter-totter, a tree house, and monkey bars.

★ The Kennedys lost two children: their first child, a stillborn daughter, and their son Patrick.

★ First dad John F. Kennedy loved to read bedtime stories to his kids when he was home to tuck them in.

★ The Kennedys' nanny was named Maud Shaw. She was employed by Jacqueline Kennedy after Caroline was born and stayed with the family for more than six years.

★ When the Kennedys took over the White House, Mrs. Kennedy had Margaret Truman's old room and suite converted to a small kitchen and dining room for John and Caroline. She thought that their food got cold when it was carried all the way from the main kitchen in the basement.

★ When Caroline arrived at the White House, she found a huge snowman waiting to greet her at the front door. The head gardener built it especially for her.

★ Caroline's dad, JFK, called her Buttons.

★ Caroline's three children are named Rose, Tatiana, and John.

★ One of John's Secret Service Agents taught him how to ride a bike without training wheels.

★ John Jr. was dubbed "John-John" by the press; however this was because they heard his dad calling him one day from the swimming pool. The president yelled out, "John . . . John." He said his name twice because, at first, John Jr. didn't hear his dad. His own family never called him John-John.

★ Mrs. Kennedy often took John and Caroline to a place called Glen Ora from Thursday through Tuesday so they could play while no one interrupted or tried to take photos.

★ As a kid, John Jr. loved the sea. He boated a lot with his family at the Kennedy summer home.

"Children of men in public life — somewhat like the children of preachers — learn early in life that people expect them to be adults before they are even adolescents."
— Lynda Bird Johnson

Lyndon B. Johnson
(1963-1969)

# The Lyndon B. Johnsons

The Lyndon B. Johnson administration came about in 1963 because of the untimely death of John F. Kennedy. Suddenly, in the blink of an eye, America had a new president. This larger-than-life man with two daughters was certainly qualified to be our 36th president, having been a vice president and a senator for many years. However, despite all the titles he had attained, the title he most enjoyed was that of dad. Both Luci and Lynda played very important roles in the White House. They had responsibility within the entertainment schedule of the White House, but also functioned as ambassadors for their first lady mom. They often stood in for her when she was too busy or overscheduled.

## LYNDA BYRD JOHNSON ROBB

was born basically on the campaign trail on March 19, 1944, in Washington, D.C. Her dad had been a congressman for seven years by the time she was born. She wasn't really interested in politics until she was a teenager. The atmosphere in the capital

143

suddenly captivated her attention. She used to hang around her dad's office a lot in the Capitol and even gave tours. She became a first kid in a sad way when President Kennedy was killed in November 1963. She knew as she boarded the flight from Austin to Washington that her life would never be the same. Suddenly, she and her sister were thrust into the spotlight. Daily mail would pour in with suggestions for her father and the Vietnam War as well as letters for her that suggested she find a new hairstyle.

Lynda Johnson as an Azalea Queen with her father in 1961.

During her father's administration she transferred to George Washington University to be closer to the family but eventually transferred back to University of Texas and graduated there with honors and a B.A. in history. Lynda fell in love and had the White House wedding of her dreams. In the first White House wedding since the Franklin Roosevelt administration in 1942, Lynda Byrd Johnson became Mrs. Charles S. Robb on December 9, 1967. With Lynda's help and support, Charles Robb would go on to become a Virginia senator as well as its governor. Lynda Byrd Johnson would become a first lady like her mom . . . but a first lady of one of the fifty states, not all of them. The couple has three daughters.

# LUCI BAINES JOHNSON TURPIN

was born on July 2, 1947. She was the first teen to inhabit the White House in fifty years. As a child, she underwent several procedures involving clipping her tongue in order to overcome a speech impediment. She also

Luci Johnson blowing out the candles on her seventeenth birthday (1964).

President Johnson walks Luci down the aisle at her wedding (1966).

The Johnson family (1965).

went to a speech pathologist for years to speak properly. Luci had headaches and poor grades as a teen, though she studied very hard. She had 20/20 vision but was diagnosed with a visual perception problem that she eventuallly corrected with therapy. Pets were a big part of the Johnson White House, and Luci was the keeper of most of them. The Johnsons had several dogs through the years, but Luci had found a dog she named Yuki at a Texas gas station and persuaded her dad to keep him. There were also the two famous beagles named Him and Her and the hamsters. Once Luci's hamsters roamed freely through the White House during an important state dinner with Princess Margaret. She was attending Georgetown University in the nursing program when she fell in love. Luci married Patrick J. Nugent in the National Shrine of the Immaculate Conception on August 6, 1966. They had four children. The marriage was annulled in 1979. Luci moved to Austin and eventually married Ian Turpin in 1984. She went back to school and graduated from St. Edward's University at the age of 50. Luci remains active in her support and leadership of Volunteers for Vision, the Lyndon B. Johnson holding company, and her father's library and museum.

# FAST FACTS

★ Lynda and Luci Johnson were Brownies and Girl Scouts.

★ Both Johnson daughters married military men who served in Vietnam. Patrick Nugent was in the National Guard, Charles Robb was in the Marines.

★ Luci changed the spelling of her name from Lucy to Luci . . . because she wanted to.

★ Luci was the eighth daughter of a president to be married while her dad was president.

★ Luci's pet hamsters, named Boris and Ninotchka, produced a litter of eleven babies while in the White House.

★ Lynda's wedding ceremony was held in the East Room of the White House.

★ Luci's dad gave her a Corvette for her sixteenth birthday.

★ Luci never remembered having lunch or dinner as a family (with just her, her sister, Mom, and Dad) until the age of sixteen because her parents were so busy.

**JOHNSON**

★ Luci considered her seventeenth birthday to be the most memorable. On that day, her dad signed the Civil Rights Act.

★ Lynda and Luci sold Girl Scout cookies to all the people who worked for their dad in Congress.

★ Luci had a seven-tiered wedding cake that was eight feet tall and weighed 300 pounds.

★ Alice Roosevelt was invited to and attended both Johnson girls' weddings.

★ Lynda and Luci moved into John and Caroline Kennedy's rooms in the White House.

★ Lady Bird Johnson raised Luci's and Lynda's allowances while in the White House to five dollars per week.

"I have to have a room of my own. Nobody could sleep with Dick. He wakes up during the night, switches on the lights, speaks into his tape recorder."
— Pat Nixon

# The Nixons

## Richard M. Nixon (1969-1974)

Richard M. Nixon was the 37th president of the United States of America. He came into the White house as an experienced politician having served as a congressman, senator, vice president under Eisenhower, and presidential candidate in 1960 against a popular senator from Massachusetts named John F. Kennedy. Few people know Richard Nixon as a doting husband and father to his wife and two girls. He loved them dearly and carefully carved out time to be a presence in their lives. President Nixon was a huge sports nut. He was an avid football fan, and his favorite team was the Miami Dolphins. A few weeks before his beloved Dolphins played in Super Bowl VI, Nixon called the head coach to recommend a play. The coach didn't want to disappoint the president so he tried the play . . . it didn't work. Nixon was extremely gifted in the area of foreign affairs and strengthened the U.S. relationship with China. The country was strong and healthy under his leadership, but his presidency would be defined by scandal and cover-up. The Watergate scandal ultimately led him to resign before being impeached.

# TRICIA NIXON COX

Tricia's wedding (1971).

was born on February 21, 1946. Tricia moved into the White House with her family when she was twenty-two years old. It was as if she was American Royalty to the press. She received her own layout and cover story in two issues of *Life* magazine. Tricia married Ed Cox on June 12, 1971 in a lavish wedding in the Rose Garden of the White House. She is the only first kid to have married there. After the marriage and her dad's presidency and resignation, Tricia became a stay-at-home mom, caring for her only son, Christopher. When her son left for college, Tricia became even more involved as she served on many medical research institutions' board of directors. She is also very involved with the Nixon Presidential Library and Nixon Center. She and her husband live in New York City.

Pat Nixon cooking with
Tricia and Julie (1960).

Julie and Tricia Nixon in 1966.

The Nixon family (1953).

## JULIE NIXON EISENHOWER

was born on July 5, 1948. Julie Nixon had
already fallen in love and married when
her father was elected president. Her heart
belonged to a first-grandchild named David
Eisenhower II, grandson of Dwight D.
Eisenhower. They married on December
22, 1968 at the Marble Collegiate Church
in New York City. Julie lived in the White
House while her husband was in officer

Julie's wedding (1968).

candidates school in Rhode Island, training with the navy.

Julie discovered she was a good author and even wrote a cookbook for kids. She also
wrote a bestselling book on her mom entitled *Pat Nixon: The Untold Story*. David
had a story to tell as well about his famous grandfather President Eisenhower. Both
Julie and David are sought-after speakers and authors while finding the time to raise
their three children: Jennie, Alex, and Melanie.

# FAST FACTS

★ During Nixon's presidency, the 26th amendment to the Constitution was ratified. This changed the voting age from 21 to 18 years of age.

★ First Lady Pat Nixon visited 83 countries while her husband was president.

★ The Nixons were a very close and tight-knit family.

★ The first Sunday after inauguration, the Nixons held a worship service in the East Room of the White House. Dr. Billy Graham led the service.

★ Mrs. Nixon gave up a college scholarship offer to take care of her sick father. When he died she went to college and worked several part-time jobs and paid for her own tuition.

★ Tricia weighed 7 pounds when she was born.

★ When Tricia was born, her mom was so sure that she was going to be a boy that she had crocheted her a blue blanket. She had made a pattern on it that spelled out Richard.

★ Three weeks after Tricia was born, her mom, Pat Nixon, left her with her paternal grandmother, Hannah Nixon, and went on the campaign trail with her husband.

★ Tricia and her sister, Julie, went to public school in Washington, D.C., when their dad was vice president. Tricia went up to fifth grade in public school. Mrs. Nixon changed them to the Sidwell Friends coeducational private Quaker school in 1958. It took them several years to catch up. They remember doing homework until 10 or 11 at night.

★ Tricia was in politics in college. She was elected class president for her junior class.

★ Tricia was a European history major in college.

★ Tricia had a Yorkshire terrier dog named Pasha.

★ Tricia was a member of the academic honor society at Finch College in New York City.

★ Tricia and her husband, Ed Cox, were engaged two years before their parents knew.

★ When Tricia's then fiancé asked for her father's blessing on their impending marriage, Ed was said to have been very nervous and "white as a sheet."

★ The engagement ring that Ed gave Tricia had been his maternal grandmother's.

★ Alice Roosevelt Longworth attended Tricia's wedding. Other White House brides who also attended were Luci and Lynda Johnson.

★ Tricia and her husband honeymooned in Camp David.

★ Julie weighed 9 pounds 6 ounces when she was born.

★ Julie had to study very hard in high school. Her mom typed all of her research papers.

★ Julie was close to her father, and he was never a disciplinarian. She labeled him a "pushover" or "cream puff" parent.

★ Julie labels her first mom as the disciplinarian. Not harsh, just consistent, no yelling. Both girls note that she simply used "the look."

★ Julie had a pet poodle named Vicky.

★ Julie and David Eisenhower were married 29 days before her dad took office and before they graduated from college.

★ David's grandmother was so excited about their marriage that she gave David her own mother's wedding ring that she had worn for her entire 63-year marriage. David gave it to Julie when he proposed and she loved it.

★ Julie and David were married in Norman Vincent Peale's church.

★ David's grandparents were both hospitalized during their wedding. They made arrangements for them to watch the wedding on a closed-circuit television in Walter Reed Hospital. Mamie Eisenhower finally came clean with the family seven years later that the reception had failed and they saw nothing but static.

★ Julie and Tricia disagreed about how their famous father would be portrayed politically at his museum and with some of his presidential papers. There were funding issues because the Richard Nixon Library is privately funded as oppose to the other presidential libraries.

# The Fords

President Ford with his wife, Betty, and four children (1974).

## Gerald R. Ford (1974-1977)

erald R. Ford was never supposed to be our 38th president of the United States. He wasn't even supposed to be the vice president for Richard Nixon. Richard Nixon's vice president, Spiro Agnew, resigned because he had been accused of bribery. In a dash to find a vice president, Nixon chose a congressman from Michigan by the name of Gerald Ford. Soon after that, Nixon was about to be impeached for his involvement in Watergate. He resigned, and Gerald Ford became president. Ford made history: He never was elected to the office of president or vice president. He came to the White House in the midst of a crisis. The crimes of Watergate had tarnished the image of the Oval Office as well as the image of the nation in the eyes of Americans and other world powers. Ford had to get his country back on track. His first act was an unselfish one; he pardoned Nixon of all crimes involving the Watergate scandal. Despite the criticism he received for the Nixon pardon, Ford pressed on and the nation became stronger and regained respect for him. He and his wife, Betty, had four children.

# MICHAEL GERALD FORD

was born on March 14, 1950. When his father became the president, Michael was a 23-year-old student at Gordon Conwell Theological Seminary working on his master's degree. He was already married to a woman named Gayle Brumbaugh. Michael has a successful career and was even appointed the director of student affairs at his alma mater, Wake Forest University, in 1981. Michael and Gayle have three kids and are now grandparents. Today Michael is a minister and is in charge of student development at Wake Forest University.

# JOHN "JACK" GARDNER FORD

was born on March 16, 1952. Jack was fascinated with his father's political achievements and encouraged his dad to go even higher in the political ranks.

Jack enjoyed the perks of his father's presidency, including dating celebrities, meeting famous musicians, and the constant attention of the media. In 1985, he cofounded an extremely prosperous business called California InfoTech, which provides electronic information kiosks to malls across the country. He settled down and married

President and Mrs. Ford seated with Susan, Steven, Jack, Michael, and his wife, Gayle, behind them from left to right.

Juliann Felando in 1989. Jack tried his hand at politics, serving as the executive director of the host committee for the Republican Convention in San Diego, California. He presently lives with his wife and two sons in California.

# STEVEN MEIGS FORD

was born on May 19, 1956. He was raised in Washington, D.C, as his father climbed the political ladder. After graduating from high school, Steve had been accepted to Duke University but decided to take a one-year break and try ranching in Montana. Steven truly loved and enjoyed it. After his time as a rancher, he attended Utah State

Steven Ford riding a bronco for a charity event in 1976.

University and California Polytechnical Institute. He became a successful actor starring as Andy Richards in *The Young and the Restless*, Meg Ryan's boyfriend in *When Harry Met Sally*, and dozens of other films, including *Eraser* with Arnold Schwarzenegger. He also owns his own racehorses and is in demand as a motivational speaker across the nation. Steven is on the board of directors for the Gerald R. Ford Museum. Steven has never been married and has no children.

# SUSAN ELIZABETH FORD VANCE BALES

was born July 6, 1957. She was raised in Washington, D.C., like every one of her brothers, but was the only Ford first kid to actually live at 1600 Pennsylvania Avenue. Susan thoroughly enjoyed the White House and despite all the Secret Service and the press coverage she managed to be a student at Mount Vernon College,

Susan Ford washing her car at the White House (1975).

Susan with her parents and golden retriever, Liberty (1975).

write an article for *Seventeen* magazine, and become a professional photographer. After her father's presidency, she attended the University of Kansas and her photography career blossomed. She has taken pictures for *Ladies' Home Journal*, *Newsweek*, *Jaws 2*, and many other projects. In 1979, she married one of her dad's Secret Service Agents named Charles Vance, and they had two daughters. They later divorced, and Susan remarried an attorney named Vaden Bales. She wrote a book that was popular with mystery readers across the country. Susan now lives with her husband and their children near Albuquerque, New Mexico. She is a popular motivational speaker and serves as the chairman of the Betty Ford Center.

Breakfast with the Fords (1973).

# FAST FACTS

★ The Fords were at the emergency room a lot when their boys were little. There were accidents, bitten-through lips, smashed fingers, drunk bottles of teething syrup, broken bones, etc.

★ Betty Ford once coached a flag football game between her husband's Secret Servicemen and her family's Secret Servicemen.

★ Betty Ford made her children make their own beds every day. This included when they lived at the White House.

★ The Fords once had a pet alligator that lived in their backyard. The Ford boys would feed it with their boxing gloves on.

★ The Fords are all great skiers. They began skiing as a family in Michigan, then tried Utah and Colorado. Vail, Colorado, became their favorite coveted family get away for skiing.

★ When Michael was nineteen, he went hiking with friends in the Adirondack Mountains and got lost in a snowstorm. The group containing Michael had to be rescued.

★ President Ford spoke at Michael's graduation from seminary.

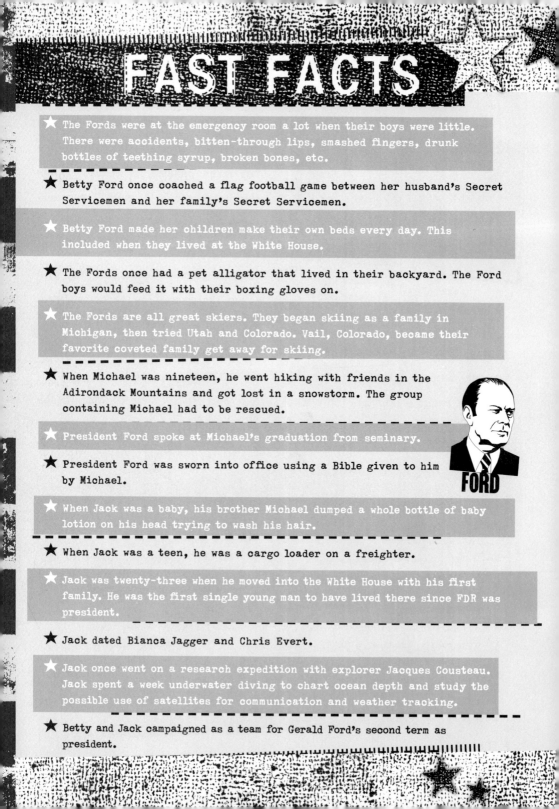

FORD

★ President Ford was sworn into office using a Bible given to him by Michael.

★ When Jack was a baby, his brother Michael dumped a whole bottle of baby lotion on his head trying to wash his hair.

★ When Jack was a teen, he was a cargo loader on a freighter.

★ Jack was twenty-three when he moved into the White House with his first family. He was the first single young man to have lived there since FDR was president.

★ Jack dated Bianca Jagger and Chris Evert.

★ Jack once went on a research expedition with explorer Jacques Cousteau. Jack spent a week underwater diving to chart ocean depth and study the possible use of satellites for communication and weather tracking.

★ Betty and Jack campaigned as a team for Gerald Ford's second term as president.

★ Steven worked in Alaska when he was twelve years old. He went with his dad on a political campaign trip. He befriended some people who operated a hunting camp. He worked there for two different summers.

★ Betty Ford used to set her clock to remind her to tune in and watch Steven on the soap opera *The Young and the Restless*.

★ Steven acted in 35 total films.

★ Steven struggled with alcoholism and went into treatment at his famous first mom's clinic, the Betty Ford Clinic.

★ Steven is single and lives in California. He is a sought after speaker and entertainer.

★ Betty Ford never let Susan's brothers babysit for her because they would go to the fuse box and turn out all the lights to scare her. They would hide under her bed until after she had said her prayers and crawled into bed. As soon as the light was out, they would jump out from under the bed and grab her, making her scream.

★ Susan hosted her senior prom at the White House. This was the first and only high school prom ever held at the Executive Mansion.

★ Susan's first dad gave the commencement address at her high school, the Holton-Arms Girls School, when she graduated.

★ The press constantly covered Susan. Once the press reported that she was engaged to rock star Rod Stewart. She had only attended his concert and met him backstage.

★ Susan has been on many boards, including her children's school, Bosque Prep School, Betty Ford Center (she is now the head), and was a spokesperson for National Breast Cancer Awareness Month.

★ Susan was interested in photojournalism and studied with one of her dad's White House photographers.

★ Susan has the highest regard for her mom, Betty. She fondly recalls her mom always putting her and her brothers first and being present at everything they were involved in.

★ As a kid, Susan enjoyed sports, dance, and photography.

★ Susan admits she didn't get amazing grades in school and didn't enjoy reading.

★ Susan wrote a monthly column as a seventeen-year-old in the White House for *Seventeen* magazine.

President Carter with his wife, Rosalynn, and family (sometime between 1977 and 1980).

# The Carters

### Jimmy Carter (1977-1981)

Jimmy Carter succeeded Gerald Ford as the 39th president of the United States. America noticed that with the Carters came a sense of the ordinary. After all he was straight off the family peanut farm in Plains, Georgia. The Carters chose to walk their inaugural parade route rather than drive, and they turned down all the thermostats in the Executive Mansion to save energy. When they were cold, they simply wore sweaters. They did away with the presidential yacht and sent their school-age child to public school rather than private. Jimmy Carter considered his wife, Rosalynn, a full partner in marriage and his administration. She often attended cabinet meetings and gave him advice and suggestions. The president and first lady enjoyed lots of activities together like exercising, fishing, long walks, etc.

The Carters walking the inaugural parade route (1977).

Jimmy Carter loved classical music and had it piped right into his office. President Carter is perhaps remembered the most for negotiating a peace treaty between Egypt and Israel at Camp David. He is also known for starting Habitat for Humanity, a huge Christian ministry that builds homes for the needy.

## JOHN "JACK" WILLIAM CARTER

was born on July 3, 1947. He was considered very bright and eager to learn. Jack served in the Vietnam War in the navy. After the war, he went to college at Georgia Tech and eventually the University of Georgia Law School. After his college experience, Jack easily passed the Georgia state bar. He met and married Juliette Langford, also known as Judy. Jack and Judy had two children together. After his father's presidency, Jack moved to Illinois and worked for the Chicago Board of Trade. They later divorced and he currently lives in Bermuda with Elizabeth Brasfield Carter, his new wife.

## JAMES "CHIP" EARL CARTER III

From left to right: Jeff and his wife, Annette; Jack and his wife, Judy; (2nd row) Edna Landford (Judy's mother); President and Mrs. Carter; and Chip and his wife, Karen (1976).

was born on April 12, 1950. He seemed to be destined for politics, especially when he was out campaigning for John F. Kennedy's 1960 election when he was just ten years old. He helped his dad get elected to the Georgia senate, Georgia gubernatorial office, and the presidency. He married Caron Griffin in between his dad's campaigns and had a son. His first marriage ended in divorce during his father's presidency. He soon married again to Ginger Hodges and had a daughter. There were many rumors that Chip might get into politics himself. Instead he settled down and managed the famous

Jeff Carter (1976).

Carter peanut farm for a while, until he became involved with work at the Carter Center. In 2000, he was the new president of the Friendship Force, a group focused on erasing stereotypes across the globe. After his second divorce, he got married for a third time to Becky Payne. They live in Georgia.

## DONNELL JEFFREY "JEFF" CARTER

was born on August 18, 1952. Jeff was almost unknown to the press and was not followed by the media. As a first kid, this must have been a relief. While his father was president, he was already married to the love of his life, Annette Davis, and was a student at George Washington University. He and Annette both moved into 1600 Pennsylvania Avenue. Soon after his graduation from GWU in computer cartography, Jeff and one of his professors created Computer Mapping Consultants. His company has grown into an extremely successful business. He currently lives near Atlanta with Annette and three kids. He is the ultimate story of having a successful and normal life as a first kid.

## AMY LYNN CARTER WENTZEL

was the only Carter girl, born on October 19, 1967, in Plains, Georgia. She was enrolled in public school to prove that the public education system was good enough even for a president's daughter.

Amy Carter sitting at her father's desk in 1977.

President Carter with Amy and Jason (grandson) in their treehouse on the South Lawn of the White House (1977).

Amy Carter's wedding (1996).

She couldn't play outside at recess though, because her teachers were worried about something happening to her. Everything she did was scrutinized, and the press constantly ridiculed her and oftentimes made fun of her looks. After her father's presidency, Amy returned to Plains with her family. Eventually, she went to Brown University and earned her master's degree at Tulane University in fine arts and art history. Amy is a terrific artist and has illustrated two of her father's books. While working in an Atlanta bookstore, she met the love of her life, Jim Wentzel. They got married in her late grandmother Lillian Carter's home on September 1, 1996. They lived in New Orleans for a while but then moved to Atlanta with their one son, Hugo James Wentzel. She has become more active with the Carter Center and has traveled around the globe with her brother Chip's Friendship Force. Because her childhood was so invaded by the press, as an adult she never grants interviews.

# FAST FACTS

★ In the 1950s, Jimmy Carter and his family returned to Plains, Georgia, to help run the family peanut farm. He turned the farm into a multimillion-dollar business.

★ The Carter family had a dog named Grits while in the White House. Grits hated their cat named Misty Malarky Ying Yang.

★ The Carter family had a special acronym code they used with one another. It was ILYTG which stood for "I Love You The Goodest!"

★ Jimmy Carter was a Boy Scout leader when his sons were growing up.

★ After Vietnam Jack returned to college earning a degree in nuclear physics. He also went on to law school.

★ Jack ran for the U.S. Senate for Nevada in 2006.

CARTER

★ When Chip was five years old, he and his family were camping and he caught a huge fish with a little stick pole. It was five times as large as the fish his fisherman father had caught. This picture still has a prized place on the mantel.

★ Chip once got in trouble and was sent to the principal's office in school for throwing a chair at his teacher. The teacher had said "good" when the announcement was made that JFK had been shot.

★ Integration came to Plains, Georgia, when Chip was in high school.

★ Chip worked for his famous first dad when he was president. He also had worked for the Democratic National Convention as well as his hometown city council.

★ When the situation with Iran worsened during his dad's presidency, some Iranian students on a Texas college campus attacked Chip. Secret service protected him, and he was not hurt.

★ Jeff loved astronomy and used his telescope from the White House roof outside the solarium.

★ Jeff sometimes called the Smithsonian service "dial-a-phenomenon" to find out what was going on with the stars and planets.

★ Jeff's famous first dad made the cradle for his first child.

★ Jeff helps at the Carter Center training the student interns on the center's work with other countries. He is an expert on Indonesia and many other Asian countries.

★ Amy spent lots of time with her grandmothers as a baby. Her parents were campaigning endlessly.

★ Amy's brothers chose her name.

★ Amy used a chair and sofa set in her White House bedroom that had been given to Caroline Kennedy during her father's presidency. It had never been used.

★ In addition to Misty Malarky Ying Yang and Grits, Amy had other pets as well. She had another dog-named J.B. (Jet Black) and a parakeet named Blueberry.

★ Amy and her family loved to bowl and watch movies in the White House.

★ Amy performed with her violin class in the White House.

★ A White House staffer built Amy a tree house on the South Lawn of the White House.

★ Amy's room in the White House had also been the room of Caroline Kennedy, Luci Johnson, and Tricia Nixon.

★ Amy loved to read.

★ Amy and her friends sometimes had fun parties at the White House and would tell ghost stories in the Lincoln Bedroom.

★ Once Amy was at a pet show and a large elephant broke loose and ran toward her. The secret service lifted her out of the way just before the elephant crashed through the fence.

★ Amy took violin lessons while living at the White House. Her mom took them with her, too.

★ Amy was a page in the U.S. Senate when she was on summer vacation from high school.

★ Amy has a master's degree in fine arts.

# The Reagans

## Ronald Reagan (1981-1989)

onald Reagan was America's 40th president. He was often called the Great Communicator for his skill and poise as an orator and writer. He and his wife, Nancy, made the White House glamorous. After all they were from Hollywood. Reagan is hailed for bringing down the Berlin Wall and beginning the end to the Cold War. President Reagan was also a dad to Maureen and Michael from his first marriage to Jane Wyman and to Patti and Ron Jr. from his marriage to Nancy. The Reagan first kids were already adults when their famous father became commander in chief, but they would continue to make his world a little more colorful.

## MAUREEN ELIZABETH REAGAN FILIPPONE SILLS REVELL

was born on January 4, 1941. She was ambitious at a young age. Maureen eventually went to Marymount College. She dropped out and became an actress, but Maureen was a political activist at heart. She was elected cochairman of the Republican

National Committee. After that, she became the U.S representative to the United Nations, speaking out for women. During her travels, Maureen and her third husband, Dennis Revell, adopted a Ugandan girl in 1994. When her famous father had Alzheimer's, she tirelessly raised money for a cure. She did all this work on her dad's behalf despite having advanced-stage melanoma, a deadly type of skin cancer. She eventually died of this disease on August 8, 2001, at the age of sixty.

Maureen Reagan (1975).

## MICHAEL EDWARD REAGAN

was born on March 18, 1945. His parents, Jane Wyman and Ronald Reagan, adopted Michael three days later. He and his sister Maureen were later in childhood sent to different boarding schools and camps. At the schools, he often was in trouble just to get his parents' attention. He was offered scholarships as an athlete but turned

President Reagan with Jane Wyman, Maureen, and Michael (circa 1945).

them down to live a little and get married. His marriage to Pamela Putnam didn't last, and he later attended Arizona State University. He was a businessman for a time in an airplane machinery company. Eventually, he got into radio where he has found success hosting a radio talk show. It is broadcast on more than 200 different stations. In 1975, Michael married Colleen Sterns. They have two children.

# PATRICIA ANN "PATTI DAVIS" REAGAN GRILLEY

was born on October 21, 1952. Patti was the first child of Nancy and Ronald Reagan. As a child, she went to boarding school, while her father started his political career. She went to Northwestern University but left college to become an actress and model. Considered the family rebel, she did not stop rebelling when her dad became president. For effect, she changed

Patti Davis and Ron with their parents (circa 1955).

her last name (Reagan) to her mother's maiden name (Davis). Her continual drug use eventually led to anorexia. Patti married Paul Grilley. Along her journey, she realized she wanted to change her life for the better. She has written several books in tribute to her famous parents. She currently travels across the country speaking and discussing the value of family and forgiveness. She is divorced and has no children.

# RONALD "RON" PRESCOTT REAGAN

Ron Reagan sliding down a stair banister (circa 1967).

was born on May 20, 1958. He was attending Yale when he had the opportunity to become a professional ballet dancer. He was ridiculed constantly for pursuing his dream, but that didn't slow him down. He joined a dance troupe and traveled making sufficient money. After a few years with the dancing group, Ron married a fellow dancer named Doria Palmieri. Ron then quit dancing to pursue journalism. He is currently a respected journalist and known as a TV personality. He remains close with his mom and actively campaigns for stem cell research. He enjoys life in Seattle with his wife (who's now a psychologist). He has three cats and no children.

# FAST FACTS

★ Ronald and Nancy Reagan teamed up long before being the president and first lady. They starred in a movie together in their Hollywood days called *Hellcats of the Navy*.

★ Ronald Reagan was the first president to wear contact lenses and a hearing aid.

★ The Reagans loved to go horseback riding. They did this often at their California ranch.

★ Maureen was interested in politics at an early age. She watched primaries and political convention speeches on television.

★ Maureen campaigned for Dwight Eisenhower at age eleven. She wore an "I Like Ike" button to school and convinced all the schoolchildren to go home and tell their parents to vote for Eisenhower.

★ Maureen declared herself a Republican before her famous father did. Ronald Reagan was a Democrat until the Nixon campaign.

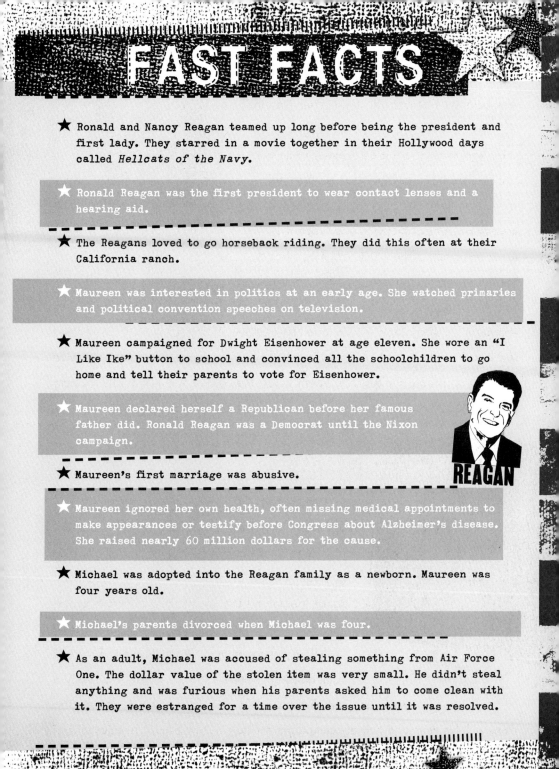

REAGAN

★ Maureen's first marriage was abusive.

★ Maureen ignored her own health, often missing medical appointments to make appearances or testify before Congress about Alzheimer's disease. She raised nearly 60 million dollars for the cause.

★ Michael was adopted into the Reagan family as a newborn. Maureen was four years old.

★ Michael's parents divorced when Michael was four.

★ As an adult, Michael was accused of stealing something from Air Force One. The dollar value of the stolen item was very small. He didn't steal anything and was furious when his parents asked him to come clean with it. They were estranged for a time over the issue until it was resolved.

★ Michael is the most conservative politically of all the Reagan children.

★ Michael is a sought-after speaker as well as an author.

★ Patti appeared with her parents on television commercials when she was very young.

★ Patti was considered wild and uncontrollable as a teenager.

★ As a young adult, Patti rarely saw any of her family.

★ Patti wrote an autobiography that exposed the Reagan family as dysfunctional. Her parents were painted in a terrible light, especially her mother.

★ Ron was a fun-loving and easygoing child.

★ Ronald used to put his son Ron on his shoulders and hurl him down to the deep end of the pool. There was lots of swimming in the Reagan family.

★ Ron was as close to his parents as he could be. He always said that Ronald and Nancy were in a circle that no one else could enter . . . not even their own children.

★ Ron attended Yale for a semester and then went to the Joffrey School of Dance in New York.

★ Ron danced in a skit in his underwear on *Saturday Night Live*.

★ Ron argued with his dad about his secret service protection as a student. He told his dad that he was interfering with his life.

★ Ron considers himself liberal but is really a nonpolitical-type person.

★ Ron eulogized his famous dad at his funeral in Simi Valley, California.

> *"The greatest gift a parent can give a child is unconditional love. As a child wanders and strays, finding his bearings, he needs a sense of absolute love from a parent. There's nothing wrong with tough love, as long as the love is unconditional."*
> — *George H. W. Bush*

# The George H. W. Bushes

President Bush with his wife, Barbara, and children (left to right): Doro, George W., Neil, Marvin, and Jeb (circa 1960s).

## George H. W. Bush (1989-1993)

George Herbert Walker Bush was the 41st president of the United States. First on the list was to be the youngest pilot in U.S. Navy history. In fact, when his plane was shot down into the ocean, he had to wait three hours to be rescued. He was injured and bleeding and in shark-infested waters. He was eventually rescued, but only after the longest hours of his life. He was also ambassador to the United Nations, congressman, CIA director, and vice president to Ronald Reagan for eight years. Despite all of his political accomplishments, what he enjoyed the most was being a husband to his wife, Barbara, and watching as his children grew and became successful in their own right. Two were governors of large states, and one of those ended up in the White House! George and Barbara are proud parents but make no mistake, they were not pushovers, and the Bush kids had rules and chores like all kids. Now that all of his kids have grown up George now enjoys jumping out of airplanes. (Don't worry, he has a parachute!)

George H. W. Bush with his mother and two children, George W., and Robin (1953).

# GEORGE WALKER BUSH

was born on July 6, 1946. George W. was a HUGE baseball fan. He went to hundreds of baseball games as a kid and was determined to become the next Willie Mays. George W. started out strong quickly becoming the star catcher on his Little League team (the first president to ever to be a Little Leaguer). His autographed baseball card collection to this day stands at more than 250. George eventually graduated from Yale University (his father's alma mater). After graduation, he decided to go into the National Guard and, then went to Harvard Business School for his MBA. He ran for Congress and didn't win, but George did not give up. He decided to follow his childhood passion and became part owner and executive manager of the Texas Rangers. The Bush bloodline could not be escaped, and he entered into the political arena again. This time he ran for governor of his adopted home state of Texas. George was so popular as governor of the Lone Star State that he was elected to two terms. He won the support and nomination of the Republican Party and faced Al Gore (the two-term vice president under Bill Clinton). In one of the closest elections in history, George W. Bush became our 43rd president. He now lives in Texas with his wife, Laura. They have twin daughters.

# PAULINE ROBINSON "ROBIN" BUSH

was born on December 20, 1949. Robin was born only months after Barbara Bush's mother died in a car accident. One day, Robin asked her mom if she could stay in bed or lie on the grass instead of playing. She was tired, pale, and lacking energy. Her mom was a little worried because she was usually so full of spirit and bounce. The pediatrician had to tell George and Barbara that Robin had leukemia. The doctor informed them that Robin had only few more weeks to live. She instructed them to make Robin comfortable and enjoy the time they had left with her. Robin was taken to the renowned Memorial Sloan-Kettering Cancer Center in New York where she endured a series of excruciating tests. For seven long and difficult months, Robin endured. The cancer medicine was very painful and strong, causing internal bleeding. Surgery was soon necessary or she would die. The operation was unsuccessful. Robin Bush died on October 11, 1953, only forty-one days before her fourth birthday.

Bush family photo (undated).

# JOHN ELLIS "JEB" BUSH

was born on February 11, 1953. He and his brothers were famous in their neighborhood for playing so rough and wild that they constantly were visiting the emergency room. Jeb would survive his childhood and graduate Phi Beta Kappa from the University of Texas. He fell in love with a girl named Columba Garnica Gallo. Jeb later became the governor of Florida. At the moment, his political career is on hiatus due to the fact that Jeb was elected to two terms as the Florida governor and could not run for a third, because of term limits. Jeb and his wife, Columba, have three children.

George W. and Jeb Bush at a campaign rally in Florida (2004).

President Bush with his four sons (1970).

# NEIL MALLON BUSH

was born on January 22, 1955. As a child Neil got all As and was considered ahead of the class in everything. To his mom's surprise, Neil was discovered to be dyslexic. He eventually worked through the limitation and learned how to read and write. Neil went on to Tulane University. After he graduated, he moved to the mountains of Colorado with his wife, Sharon. Neil became the director of a savings and loan corporation. When the savings and loan he worked for failed, he moved to Houston where he is currently an investment consultant and in charge of a highly regarded educational software company called Ignite! Learning. Neil and Sharon Bush had three children together. After a 23-year marriage, Neil and Sharon divorced and he married Maria Andrew in 2004. Neil and his wife live in Houston, Texas.

# MARVIN PIERCE BUSH

was born on October 22, 1956. He graduated from the University of Virginia, and then fell in love with Margaret Molster. They got married on June 13, 1981 when Marvin was twenty-four years old. He was athletic and strong and in fit condition. He began experiencing abdominal pain and bleeding and lost more than forty pounds. After many trips to the hospital and multiple tests, doctors diagnosed Marvin with colitis. With the love and support of his family and friends, he proceeded with an operation and has regained his health. After that, his career has been on the rise as he has worked for three major investment firms until he started his own successful business called Winston Partners L.B. He has spent hundreds of hours volunteering to encourage others who will undergo the same colon operation. He lives in Virginia with his wife. They have two kids.

# DOROTHY "DORO" WALKER BUSH LEBLOND KOCH

was born on August 18, 1959. Doro was a teenager when her father's political career was on the rise. She graduated from Boston College. She married William LeBlond while her father was vice president, but the marriage soon ended in divorce. When her father was president, she married Robert Koch at Camp David. She is the only first kid ever to marry at Camp David. Doro has had very interesting jobs, including caterer, travel agent, tourism promoter, author, and bookkeeper. She lives in Maryland with her husband and four kids.

Doro Bush with her father in Maine (1980).

# FAST FACTS

★ George H. W. Bush met his wife, Barbara, at a school dance where friends introduced them.

★ Former president George H. W. Bush is related to his own former vice president, Dan Quayle. They are distant cousins (tenth).

★ The Bush family dog that lived in the White House with them became famous for her spots and writing books. The springer spaniel's name was Millie.

★ George Bush once gave his wife Barbara twenty-four pairs of her favorite sneakers in all different colors for her birthday. They were Keds. Sometimes Barbara wears different colors on each foot for variety.

★ George Herbert Walker was George H. W. Bush's namesake and grandfather. He purchased Walker's Point at the beginning of the 1900s. Several years later, the big house was added. George H. W. Bush bought Walker's Point from his extended family when he was vice president. It continues to be the famous Bush family compound, gathering place, relaxing spot, etc. in Kennebunkport, Maine.

★ George W. usually went to Camp Longhorn for the entire month of July as a kid.

★ George W. once used an ink pen to draw sideburns, a mustache, and beard on his face in his fourth-grade classroom. He got in trouble.

**BUSH**

★ George W. attended public schools from grade school through junior high.

★ George W.'s dad helped coach his Little League baseball team.

★ George W. rode his bike a lot as a kid, and he and his friends sometimes shot frogs with BB guns.

★ George W. ran for president of his eighth-grade class and won!

★ George W. once had a date with Tricia Nixon while her father was president.

★ George W. and his wife, Laura, were in the same school for seventh grade.

★ There are two things named for Robin Bush: the Robin Bush Children's Activity Room in the Barbara Bush Library located in Spring, Texas, and the Robin Bush Child and Adolescence Clinic at M.D. Anderson Cancer Center in Houston, Texas.

★ When Jeb was a kid, he was diagnosed with a rare bone disease. Fortunately, it turned out to just be an infection in his heel.

★ In high school, Jeb participated in a student-exchange type program in Mexico. He met his future wife there.

★ Jeb Bush and his brother George W. were the second pair of brothers to serve as governors at the same time. Winthrop and Nelson Rockefeller did the same thing from 1967 to 1971 as governors of Arkansas and New York.

★ Neil earned an undergraduate degree in international economics and graduate degree in business administration.

★ Neil's brothers and sister called him "Mr. Perfect" growing up.

★ Marvin choose the blond cocker spaniel puppy given to Barbara Bush for her forty-eighth birthday.

★ Marvin's whole family was in China when he graduated from high school. His mom couldn't miss his graduation and surprised him by flying in just in time!

★ Marvin loves to fish with his dad at Kennebunkport.

★ Marvin and his wife adopted two children, Marshall and Charles Walker.

★ Marvin gave his dad Ranger, which was a puppy of Millie's.

★ Marvin campaigned with his mom a lot during his dad's reelection campaign.

★ Doro was the Bush family princess.

★ Doro went to the National Cathedral School in Washington, D.C.

★ Doro lived with her mom and dad in New York at the official U.N. ambassador's residence in the Waldorf-Astoria Hotel. Her brothers were away at school.

# Presidents Who Were U.S. Senators Before They Were President

James Monroe — Virginia

John Quincy Adams — Massachusetts

Andrew Jackson — Tennessee

Martin Van Buren — New York

William Henry Harrison — Ohio

John Tyler — Virginia

Franklin Pierce — New Hampshire

James Buchanan — Pennsylvania

Andrew Johnson — Tennessee

Benjamin Harrison — Indiana

Warren G. Harding — Ohio

Harry S Truman — Missouri

John F. Kennedy — Massachusetts

Lyndon B. Johnson — Texas

Richard M. Nixon — California

Barack H. Obama — Illinois

# The Clintons

### William J. Clinton (1993-2001)

William J. Clinton was elected our 42nd president. Suddenly, the Oval Office seemed young again. Youth radiated almost like it did with John F. Kennedy. Bill Clinton had an amazing education, including Georgetown University, Oxford University, and Yale Law School. His résumé includes titles such as lawyer, law professor, Arkansas attorney general, and the governor of Arkansas. He is the only U.S. president to be a Rhodes scholar. It is true he is academically gifted but also musically gifted as well. He plays the saxophone. President and Mrs. Clinton set high boundaries for the press around their only daughter, Chelsea, who was twelve when they moved into the White House. They wanted her to have a normal upbringing and to this day, her private life is somewhat shrouded. Chelsea's parents are dynamic public servants. In 2000, Chelsea's mom was actually elected to the Senate while her dad was still serving as president. On January 20, 2007, Hillary officially announced her candidacy for the Democratic Party presidential nomination. Early on, she was

Chelsea Clinton at a voting booth in 1986 with her father.

considered the front-runner. Hillary was not the first woman to run for president. Victoria Woodhull ran for president in 1872 as the candidate for the Equal Rights Party. However, Hillary had the best chance to win. In the end, fellow candidate Barack Obama, who went on to become the 44th president of the United States, narrowly defeated her for the Democratic nomination. Though the outcome was not what Hillary had hoped for, she was given the esteemed position of Secretary of State in President Obama's Cabinet.

# CHELSEA VICTORIA CLINTON

was born on February 27, 1980. Chelsea was brought home from the hospital to the governor's mansion. She was born right into the political life. Though she was living in a very political and powerful family, she was just a normal kid in public school, who was really smart and even skipped a grade. After the election, the Clintons came out with a new set of rules that included absolutely no interviews, and that Chelsea would attend private school. The Clintons held fast to their rule that Chelsea was not allowed to be photographed by the press. She was able to be a kid; she even got to take ballet. Chelsea graduated from high school and went to Stanford University in California. Yes, her Secret Service

Chelsea performing in "The Nutcracker" at George Mason University (1996).

agents went with her to college. Her parents insisted on the same privacy on the West Coast that Chelsea had been allowed on the East Coast. Like normal parents, these first parents even helped her move in her dorm room. Chelsea assisted her mom with her Senate campaign and shortly thereafter graduated from Stanford. After that, she followed in her father's footsteps and went to graduate school at Oxford University. Chelsea has a bright future ahead of her because of her résumé, IQ, and last name.

President Clinton, Chelsea, and Socks (cat) in the Oval Office (1994).

The Clintons at Stanford University (1997).

# FAST FACTS

★ Bill Clinton bought a house and then proposed to Hillary Clinton. They were married in the living room of that house.

★ Hillary Clinton was the first, first lady to run for office and win.

★ The Clintons met at Yale Law School. They are both lawyers.

★ *People* magazine named Chelsea Clinton as one of the "25 Most Intriguing People of 2002."

★ Chelsea attended the same private school that the Nixon daughters attended, Sidwell Friends School.

★ When Chelsea was thirteen years old, she traveled across the world with her parents to Russia.

★ Chelsea Clinton was born at II:45 p.m. CST and weighed 6 pounds I ounce.

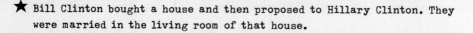

★ Chelsea was named for the title of a Judy Collins song entitled "Chelsea Morning."

**CLINTON**

★ Chelsea was the first grandchild on both sides.

★ When Chelsea was a baby and her dad was watching her, he was also watching a sports game on television and writing down a few things and answering the phones. Chelsea could not seem to get her dad's attention so she bit him on the nose.

★ Chelsea was asked as a toddler what exactly her father did for a living. Her answer was "he talks on the telephone, drinks coffee, and makes "'peeches."

★ Chelsea went to Forest Park Elementary School in Little Rock, Arkansas.

★ Chelsea played softball and volleyball as a kid.

★ Chelsea had braces as a teenager.

★ Chelsea brought four of her friends from Arkansas to the inaugural festivities when her dad was elected president. They returned to the White House for a sleepover.

★ During the inaugural sleepover, Chelsea and her friends had a scavenger hunt in the White House.

★ The Clintons cleared their schedules while in the White House to have dinner as a family as much as possible.

★ Sometimes Chelsea's mom would make her eggs in the family kitchen of the White House.

★ The secret service code names for the Clintons were Bill — Eagle, Hillary — Evergreen, and Chelsea — Energy while in the White House.

★ First dad Bill Clinton helped Chelsea with her algebra homework. If he was traveling and out of town, Chelsea would fax him the problems and they would talk on the phone about the solutions.

★ Chelsea was a star soccer player.

★ Bill Clinton often borrowed a car from his secret service while at Camp David so he could teach Chelsea to drive.

★ Chelsea's cat, Socks, became the most famous cat in America.

★ In 1997, Chelsea traveled with her mom to Africa.

★ Chelsea is an accomplished pianist.

★ Chelsea is fluent in German.

★ Chelsea was a 1997 National Merit scholar semifinalist.

★ The Clintons allowed Chelsea to make her own decision about her college choice. Though they hoped she would choose locally, she chose to go to the opposite coast.

★ Chelsea works and lives in New York.

★ The secret service agents assigned to Chelsea at Stanford were required to dress like students and lived in a dorm room near Chelsea's.

★ Chelsea is a vegetarian.

# White House Facts

Not all first kids get to live in the White House. Some first kids did not live to see their dad become president. Some first kids were already adults and out on their own when their father became the commander in chief. Even though all presidents except George Washington got to live in the White House, it is also the people's house. There are millions of people each year who pass through a guided tour of the White House. There are state functions and dinners held there. There are meetings and concerts held there and even an Easter egg roll on the lawn. See how many of these facts you are familiar with about the most famous address in the world, 1600 Pennsylvania Avenue.

The White House stretches 168 feet long.

It is almost as wide as it is long, 152 feet with porticoes.

Top to bottom height of the White House is 70 feet on the south and 60 feet 4 inches on the north.

The fence around the White House encloses 18 acres.

There are 132 rooms in the White House:

16 family/guest rooms
1 main kitchen
1 diet kitchen
1 family kitchen
35 bathrooms
1 tennis court
1 swimming pool
1 movie theater
1 jogging track
8 staircases
6 stories
3 elevators
28 fireplaces
412 doors
147 windows

The White House was the largest house in the
United States until after the Civil War.

James Hoban won the contest that was held to select
the designer of the White House.

The president's address is 1600 Pennsylvania Avenue,
NW, Washington, D.C. 20500

E-mail the president at: president@whitehouse.gov.

The phone number to the White House is 202-456-1414.

Approximately 150 staff members work in the West and
East Wings of the White House.

The chief usher of the White House has more than
100 employees to manage each day.

The chief usher's staff deal with the day-in, day-out running
of the executive mansion (dusting, cooking, maintenance, laundry, private
quarters, state floor, floral, décor).

The Easter Egg Roll is hosted on the lawn of the White House
the Monday following Easter.

People who attend the hard-boiled
Easter Egg Roll receive a souvenir wood egg.

President Bush with his wife, Laura, two daughters, and dog (2004).

# The George W. Bushes

## George W. Bush (2001-2009)

George Walker Bush was the 43rd president of the United States of America. George W. was born in Connecticut but moved to Texas as a child and rose through the ranks of Texas politics. As a young man, he was a Texas National Guard pilot who later became an oilman, owner of the Texas Rangers, and governor of Texas before becoming president of the United States. George and Laura Bush wanted a large family with lots of children. When George Bush was a new dad, he could be heard trying to comfort his crying twins by holding them and marching around the house singing the only song he knew all the words to . . . the Yale fight song. George W. Bush is only the second first kid to become president. The first was John Quincy

Adams. Unlike John Quincy Adams, George W. Bush was elected to two terms. He did not do this alone, however, because he enjoyed the love and support of his wife, Laura, and twin daughters, Jenna and Barbara. President Bush and his family own a ranch in Crawford, Texas, that was known as the Texas White House. Important meetings were held with world leaders there and it was a place of rest and relaxation for the entire Bush family. George and Laura Bush moved to Dallas, Texas, in 2009 after his term ended.

## BARBARA PIERCE BUSH

was born on November 25, 1981. Barbara was named after her famous grandma on her dad's side. She was a popular student and got good grades earning her the opportunity to go to Yale. Barbara is the fourth generation of her family to attend Yale. Barbara is described as quiet, serious, and very athletic. She played softball and cross-country in school. Despite her anonymity and shyness, she, like other first kids, was involved

Barbara Bush with her father in 2004.

in an incident with the police. The sisters were at a popular restaurant in Austin when Barbara ordered alcohol and was issued a citation for underage drinking. Following this incident, for which she had to take an alcohol awareness class, she returned to Yale and her life was quiet until her graduation. The Bush twins spoke for their father at the Republican National Convention in 2004 and campaigned during the year for dad as well. Barbara graduated from Yale with a degree in humanities and works for the Global Health Corps in New York.

Jenna Bush with her father in 2004.

# JENNA WELCH BUSH HAGER

was also born on November 25, 1981, the second fraternal twin. She went to public school until sixth grade then went to private school in junior high. Jenna was a student at a large public high school in the Texas state capital. At Stephen F. Austin High, she was involved in student council and senior-class vice president. Her freshman year of college, Jenna gave her family a scare when she was home in the governor's mansion to celebrate Christmas. She kept feeling sick and in pain. After being rushed to a nearby hospital, she had an emergency appendectomy. After graduating from high school, she chose to major in English at the University of Texas in Austin. Although a fairly serious student with her mind on her studies, Jenna was cited twice for underage drinking. She spent almost two years as a charter school elementary teacher in Washington, D.C., before interning with UNICEF in Latin America. Jenna was so inspired by the children she met, she wrote a book called *Ana's Story* in 2007. Jenna was married to Henry Hager on May 10, 2008, at her family's ranch in Crawford, Texas, with a crowd of 200 people watching. Jenna's husband, Henry, was an aide to Karl Rove, who was an important political advisor to first dad George W. Bush. Henry and Jenna honeymooned in Hawaii and are now enjoying their lives together in Baltimore, Maryland.

President Bush celebrates his victory as Texas governor with his daughters in 1994.

Jenna and Barbara at the Black Tie and Boots Ball in 2005.

The Bushes at Jenna's wedding (2008).

President Bush fishing with his
daughters in Maine (2004).

# FAST FACTS

★ President Bush loved eating grilled cheese sandwiches, egg salad sandwiches, hamburgers, and peanut butter and honey sandwiches from the White House kitchen.

★ Laura Bush was the second first lady to have earned a postgraduate degree.

★ First puppy Miss Beazley peed on the Oval Office carpet.

★ First dad George W. worked out six days a week. He preferred riding his mountain bike.

★ George W. Bush is the only president to be a dad of twins.

★ Barbara and Jenna are the only first kids to be twins.

★ Jenna and Barbara have had someone related to them in politics since they were born.

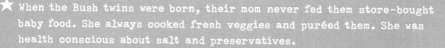

GEORGE W

★ When the Bush twins were born, their mom never fed them store-bought baby food. She always cooked fresh veggies and puréed them. She was health conscious about salt and preservatives.

★ *People* magazine interviewed the Bush daughters on the first campaign trail. They asked the twins what three things their famous first dad would bring with him if he were sent to a faraway island. They listed: A picture of the dog Barney, running shoes, and a Bible. When asked what their mother would bring, they told the reporter that she would bring Windex and cleaning supplies.

★ Jenna is named for her maternal grandmother, Jenna Welch.

★ Barbara is named for her paternal grandmother, Barbara Pierce.

★ Jenna and her sister, Barbara, introduced their first dad at the 2004 Republican National Convention.

★ Jenna traveled with her first mom on official business in 2002 to Europe.

★ Jenna loves the music of Robert Earl Keen.

★ Jenna did an internship in Argentina, Panama, and Paraguay with UNICEF.

★ Jenna was a member of Kappa Alpha Theta sorority in college.

★ Jenna was a teacher after graduating from the University of Texas at Elsie Whitlow Stokes Community Freedom Public Charter School in Washington, D.C., for almost two years.

★ Barbara took Spanish each year she was at Yale.

★ Barbara asked for a sewing machine when she was around thirteen years old. She then made her own graduation dress for her graduation from eighth grade.

★ Barbara is really good at math.

★ Barbara was the homecoming queen at Stephen F. Austin High School.

★ When Barbara was sixteen, she spent a year at the Saint Stephen's School in Rome.

★ When Jenna was sixteen she went to Spain to study. She actually lived with a family in Cádiz and was immersed in the culture.

★ Barbara and Jenna had secret service protection when they were in elementary school because their grandfather was president.

★ Barbara traveled with her first parents to Africa in 2003.

★ Barbara was born first and weighed 5 pounds 4 ounces. Jenna weighed 4 pounds 12 ounces.

★ The Bush twins used to make their dad wait in the car when he picked them up from parties because they were embarassed.

★ Laura Bush developed toxemia while she was pregnant and was on bed rest for several months at Dallas hospital. The twins were born five weeks early.

# *Living First Kids*

John Eisenhower

Caroline Bouvier Kennedy

Lynda Bird Johnson

Luci Baines Johnson

Tricia Nixon

Julie Nixon

Michael Gerald Ford

John Gardner Ford

Steven Meigs Ford

Susan Elizabeth Ford

John William Carter

James Earl Carter III

Donnell Jeffrey Carter

Amy Lynn Carter

Michael Edward Reagan

Patti Ann Reagan Davis

Ronald Prescott Reagan

George Walker Bush

John Ellis Bush

Neil Mallon Bush

Marvin Pierce Bush

Dorothy Walker Bush

Chelsea Victoria Clinton

Barbara Pierce Bush

Jenna Welch Bush

Malia Ann Obama

Natasha Obama

President Obama with his wife, Michelle, and two daughters (2008).

# The Obamas

*Barack H. Obama (2009-)*

arack H. Obama made history when he defeated John McCain to become the 44th president on November 4, 2008. This election was full of firsts that made it legendary. Here are a few: Barack Obama is the first African American elected to the presidency. His running mate, Joe Biden, is the first Roman Catholic vice president. The election was the first time two sitting senators ran against each other and the first presidential election in which campaigning lasted almost two years. President Obama was born on August 4, 1961, in Honolulu, Hawaii, only two years after it became a state. His parents divorced when he was very young. His mother, Ann Dunham, and his maternal grandparents raised him. He grew up in Hawaii except for four years when he lived with his mom in Indonesia. His interests as a youth included reading and playing basketball.

After high school, he attended Occidental College in Los Angeles, California, before transferring to Columbia University, where he earned a political science degree in 1983. Two years later, he moved to Chicago, where he worked as a community organizer to improve living conditions in poor neighborhoods. In 1991,

Obama graduated from Harvard Law School. He then returned to Chicago, where he practiced as a civil rights lawyer and taught at the University of Chicago Law School. In 1996, he ran successfully for the Illinois State Senate, where he served for eight years. He was elected to the U.S. Senate in 2004 and became the fifth African American senator from Illinois. He is the first president since Jimmy Carter to win more than 50 percent of the popular vote.

While in law school, Obama took an internship at the prestigious Chicago law firm Sidley Austin. There he met Michelle Robinson, a Princeton and Harvard graduate and an intellectual property lawyer who was assigned to mentor him. Barack and Michelle dated and eventually married in 1992. They have two daughters, Malia and Sasha.

## MALIA ANN OBAMA

was born on July 4, 1998. Malia is translated as *calm* in Hawaiian and as *queen* in Swahili. She is named after the paternal grandmother she never met, Ann Dunham. Malia is described as very social and athletic. She is involved in many different activities, including soccer, dance, drama, piano, and tennis. Malia is the oldest Obama child and is protective of her little sister, Sasha; however, they still argue just as almost all siblings do. Malia loves music, with the Jonas

Malia and Sasha playing on a tire swing in New Hampshire (2007).

Brothers topping her list of favorite bands. She also enjoys hanging out with friends and having sleepovers. Malia is just a typical preteen except that she happens to live in the White House. She goes to Sidwell Friends School in Washington, D.C.

# NATASHA OBAMA

was born on June 10, 2001. She is the baby of the Obama family. Natasha, called "Sasha," is spunky and energetic. She is involved in many different activities, including gymnastics, tennis, tap-dancing, and piano. Sasha has a passion for snow globes and collects them. Her first dad adds to her collection when he picks up unique ones on his travels. Both Malia and Sasha are very popular with the media. Sasha loves ice cream and sweets. Like her sister, Sasha goes to Sidwell Friends School.

The Obama girls relax in a hammock in New Hampshire (2007).

The Obamas in a Chicago hotel room (2004).

# FAST FACTS

★ Barack Obama won the presidential election by a 7 percent margin.

★ Barack Obama received 365 electoral votes to John McCain's 173.

★ Obama has authored two books: *Dreams from My Father* (1995) and *The Audacity of Hope* (2006).

★ Barack Obama was raised by his maternal grandmother. She died the day before the election.

★ The 2008 U.S. presidential election was the 56th consecutive quadrennial election.

★ The 2008 election was the 25th presidential election without an incumbent president on the ticket.

★ The 2008 election was the first election in 20 years that did not have a Clinton or Bush running for president.

★ Barack Obama is distantly related to both George W. Bush and Dick Cheney. He and Bush are eleventh cousins because they had the same great-great-great-great-great-great-great-great-great-great-grandparents, Samuel Hinckley and Sarah Soole of Massachusetts, in the seventeenth century. He is also distantly related to President Harry Truman.

BARACK

★ The Obama girls are the youngest first kids to live in the White House since Amy Carter in 1977.

★ Michelle was a corporate lawyer and also became involved in community service like her husband.

★ Michelle Obama shops at J. Crew.

★ Sasha and Malia have to make their beds every day in the White House. They have to do homework and clean their rooms as well.

★ Malia and Sasha love fried chicken and macaroni and cheese.

★ When the Obama girls visited the White House before their dad's inauguration, the Bush twins, Jenna and Barbara, showed them their rooms and a few ways and places to have fun in the White House. Supposedly you can slide down the Solarium ramp, and the largest cross hallway is perfect for obstacle courses.

★ Other first kids who have gone to Sidwell Friends School, where Malia and Sasha go, are Archie Roosevelt, Tricia Nixon, and Chelsea Clinton. Vice President Joe Biden's grandchildren also go there.

★ Michelle Obama attended Whitney M. Young Magnet High School in Chicago. She graduated in 1981. She was class treasurer, on student council, and in National Honor Society. Whitney Young is a public college preparatory high school.

★ President Obama promised to get his daughters a puppy at the end of the presidential campaign, win or lose.

★ The Obamas spent their 2008 Christmas vacation in Hawaii. First dad Barack grew up there and loves to bodysurf.

★ Malia is determined to use the Lincoln desk where he wrote and signed important documents. She knows it will inspire big thoughts!

★ First dad Barack Obama will NOT eat beets.

★ Michelle Obama loves grilled tilapia.

★ The first family loves take-out pizza and Mexican food.

★ All of the Obamas love healthy snacks, especially trail mix, peanuts, and veggies.

★ Sasha and Malia spent their first night in the White House going on a scavenger hunt and listening to the Jonas Brothers perform for them.

★ Michelle's mom, Marian Robinson, moved from Chicago to Washington to live with the Obamas in the White House.

# Inauguration Facts

March 4 was Inauguration Day for U.S. presidents until 1937. The Twentieth Amendment changed all that when it established that new presidents would take office at noon on January 20.

Franklin D. Roosevelt's first inaugural address contained a legendary statement still quoted today: "The only thing we have to fear is fear itself."

Another famous statement that still rings true today is from John F. Kennedy's 1961 inaugural address: "Ask not what your country can do for you, ask what you can do for your country."

Inaugurations are filled with tradition. The first tradition of Inauguration Day is for the president-elect to attend a morning worship service. This began with FDR in 1933 and all presidents-elect have followed the same tradition since then.

The oath of office as specified in the U.S. Constitution is as follows: "I do solemnly swear (or affirm) that I will faithfully execute the office of President of the United States, and will to the best of my ability, preserve, protect and defend the Constitution of the United States."

The words "so help me God" are not in the Constitution, but every president-elect has added them at the end of the oath, following in the footsteps of George Washington.

Franklin Pierce and Herbert Hoover are the only presidents-elect to use the word "affirm" rather than the word "swear" in their oaths of office.

George Washington gave the shortest inaugural address (135 words) at his second inauguration in 1793. William Henry Harrison gave the longest (8,845 words) in 1841.

The tradition of throwing the new president an inaugural ball began in 1809 with James Madison. Barack and Michelle Obama attended ten in one night!

# More Presidential Trivia

The U.S. president has an official seal. The seal's front pictures an American bald eagle carrying an olive branch in its left claw. The right claw is clutching arrows. The olive branch represents that America is a peaceful country. The arrows represent the fact that America will fight for freedom and what she believes in. You can find the seal on the back of a one-dollar bill.

The Secret Service protects our president and his family. They also protect past presidents. The Secret Service began operation on July 5, 1865, in Washington, D.C. Originally the Secret Service focused on counterfeit currency. Grover Cleveland was the first president to be protected by the service, in 1894. In 1902 two Secret Service guards were posted full- time at the White House and the Secret Service began to assume full responsibility for the protection of the U.S. president. Congress authorized protection of the first family in 1917. All former U.S. presidents began being protected by the Secret Service for a reasonable period of time due to Congress authorization in 1961. Today the Secret Service employs 6,500 personnel.

Constitutional requirements for president include the following: You must be a natural-born U.S. citizen. (In colonial times the requirements were a bit different, requiring the candidate to be either a natural-born citizen or a citizen at the time the U.S. Constitution was adopted.) You must be at least thirty-five years old. You must have lived in the United States at least fourteen years as a citizen.

The perks of being president are: Your salary is $400,000 per year, with free housing provided (the White House). You also have a place to get away to rest and relax (Camp David). When you're working, your office is not the regular old grind: It is oval in shape and decorated patriotically. You are in charge of the most powerful branch of our government (executive), and you have more responsibility than anyone else in the country.

Originally Presidents' Day was celebrated as the birthdays of two different presidents, George Washington (February 22) and Abraham Lincoln (February 12). In 1971, the third Monday in February became an official federal holiday.

# ACKNOWLEDGMENTS

## Special Thanks to:

My Savior and Lord Jesus Christ, for everything. I want to honor you in all that I do.

My mom for loving me, helping me research, and typing. I love you!
My dad for encouragement and support.
My great-grandmother, Sadie Renfro, for saving all of her *Life, Time, Good Housekeeping,* and *Ladies' Home Journal* magazines. These
had invaluable research material for me on the first kids. I love you!
My brother Nicholas, my best friend, for always waiting to play with me.
My dog, Aspen, for loving me unconditionally.

Miss JoLisa Hoover, my special friend. Thanks for reading all my manuscripts,
encouraging me, praying for me, for the ice cream and all the rides in Austin.

Mrs. Connie Harper, my former school librarian, for pulling all kinds of
hard-to-find sources for me! Thanks so much.

My editor, Brenda Murray, for introducing my work to Scholastic,
believing in me, and being so cool.

Scholastic for the amazing opportunity, and the team who worked on this book.

Mr. Jim Hornfischer, my agent, thanks for investing in me, working on my behalf,
believing in my dreams, and promising to vote for me in 2032!

My friends and family for your love and support . . . and future vote in 2032!

Barbara Cline, archivist at the LBJ Presidential Library, your assistance was invaluable.

Lynda Johnson Robb for coming in to meet me at the LBJ Library. What an honor!

George H. W. Bush Presidential Library staff for your assistance.

Stacy Davis, archivist, Gerald Ford Presidential Library, thanks for
going above and beyond the call of duty in assisting me!

All the first kids who shared their parents with America. It had to be a sacrifice.
I can't imagine not eating dinner with my mom and dad each evening.

# BIBLIOGRAPHY

## Books

Adler, Bill (ed.). *The First Mom: Wit and Wisdom of Barbara Bush.* New York: Rugged Land, 2004.

Anderson, LaVere. *Tad Lincoln: Abe's Son.* Champaign, Illinois: Garrard Publishing Company, 1971.

Angelo, Bonnie. *First Families.* New York: Harper Collins Publishers, 2007.

Anthony, Carl Sferrazza. *America's First Families.* New York: Touchstone, 2000.

Blue, Rose, and Corinne J. Naden. *The White House Kids.* Brookfield, Connecticut: The Millbrook Press, 1995.

Bourne, Miriam Anne. *The White House Children.* New York: Random House, 1979.

Bush, Barbara. *Barbara Bush: A Memoir.* New York: Scribner, 1994.

Bush, George W. *A Charge to Keep.* New York: Harper Perennial, 2001.

Caroli, Betty Boyd. *Inside The White House: America's Most Famous Home.* New York: The Reader's Digest Association, Inc., 1999.

Carter, Jimmy. *Sharing Good Times.* New York: Simon & Schuster, 2004.

Carter, Rosalynn. *First Lady from Plains.* Boston: Houghton Mifflin Company, 1994.

Clinton, Hillary Rodham. *Living History.* New York: Simon & Schuster, 2003.

Coulter, Laurie. *When John and Caroline Lived in the White House.* New York: Hyperion Books for Children, 2000.

Donald, David Herbert. *Lincoln at Home.* New York: Simon & Schuster, 2003.

Edwards, Susan. *White House Kids.* New York: Harper Perennial, 1999.

Eisenhower, Julie Nixon. *Pat Nixon: The Untold Story.* New York: Simon & Schuster, 1986.

Ford, Betty, with Chris Chase. *The Times of My Life.* New York: Harper & Row Publishers, 1978.

Fuqua, Nell. *First Pets: Presidential Best Friends.* New York: Lemon Drop Press, 2004.

————. *U.S. Presidents: Feats & Foul-Ups.* New York: Scholastic, 2003.

Gilleo, Alma. *Amy Carter: Growing Up in the White House.* Chicago: Children's Press, 1978.

Grace, Catherine O'Neill. *The White House: An Illustrated History.* New York: Scholastic, 2003.

Kessler, Ronald. *An Intimate Portrait of the First Lady: Laura Bush.* New York: Doubleday, 2006.

Koch, Doro Bush. *My Father, My President: A Personal Account of the Life of George H. W. Bush.* New York: Grand Central Publishing, 2006.

Leiner, Katherine. *First Children: Growing Up in the White House.* New York: Tambourine Books, 1996.

Lightfoot, Elizabeth. *Michelle Obama: Grace and Intelligence in a Time of Change.* New York: The Lyons Press, 2008.

Mayo, Edith P. *Smithsonian Q & A: Presidential Families.* New York: Harper Collins, 2006.

McCullough, Noah. *The Essential Book of Presidential Trivia.* New York: Random House, 2006.

Mendell, David. *Obama: A Promise of Change.* New York: Amistad, 2008.

———. *Obama: From Promise to Power.* New York: Amistad, 2008.

Obama, Barack. *The Audacity of Hope: Thoughts on Reclaiming the American Dream.* New York: Vintage, 2008.

Quinn-Musgrove, Sandra L. and Sanford Kanter. *America's Royalty.* Connecticut: Greenwood Press, 1995.

Reit, Seymour. *Growing Up in the White House: The Story of the Presidents' Children.* New York: Crowell-Collier Press, 1968.

Schweizer, Peter, and Rochelle Schweizer. *The Bushes: Portrait of a Dynasty.* New York: Doubleday, 2004.

Truman, Margaret. *First Ladies.* New York: Random House, 1996.

———. *The President's House: 1800 to the Present.* New York: Ballantine Books, 2004.

Underwood, Larry D. *All the Presidents' Children.* Lincoln, Nebraska: Dageforde Publishing, Inc. 2002.

Wead, Doug. *All the Presidents' Children.* New York: Atria Books, 2003.

## Online Sources

http://www.whitehouse.gov

http://www.potus.com

http://www.whitehousehistory.org

http://www.infoplease.com/yearbyyear.html

Bumiller, Elisabeth. "White House Letter; At Parents' Home, Bush Resumes Role of Son." *The New York Times* on the Web, July 8, 2002. http://query.nytimes.com/gst/fullpage.html?res=9901EFDD1630F93BA35754C0A9649C8B63

Reed, Julia. "Sister Act." *Vogue* magazine. Feature story on Style.com August, 2004. http://www.style.com/vogue/feature/071404.

## Personal Tours/Visits/Research

George Bush Presidential Library and Museum

The Carter Center

William J. Clinton Presidential Library and Museum

Gerald R. Ford Presidential Library and Museum

Herbert Hoover Presidential Library and Museum

Lyndon Baines Johnson Library and Museum

John F. Kennedy Presidential Library and Museum

Abraham Lincoln Library and Museum

Richard Nixon Library and Birthplace Foundation

Ronald Reagan Presidential Library and Museum

## Magazines

*Life* magazine: "All the Presidents' Children." November, 1984.

## DVD Series

*All the Presidents' Kids. Biography*/A&E Home Video 2003.

*First Daughters. Biography*/A&E. The History Channel.

# PHOTO CREDITS

Library of Congress; Page 116: Corbis; Page 117t: Hulton Archive/Getty Images; Page 117b: Corbis; Page 119tl: Library of Congress; Page 119tr: Bettmann/Corbis; Page 121t: Hulton Archive/Getty Images; Pages 121b–122: Bettmann/Corbis; Page 124: Corbis; Page 125: Bettmann/Corbis; Page 127: Hulton Archive/Getty Images; Page 128: Getty Images; Pages 129–132: Bettmann/Corbis; Page 133t: Marie Hansen/Getty Images; Pages 133b–135: Bettmann/Corbis; Page 136bl: Marie Hansen/Getty Images; Page 136br: Corbis; Page 139: Bettmann/Corbis; Page 140: The White House Historical Association; Page 141: Getty Images; Page 143: Ed Clark/Getty Images; Page 144t: Paul Schutzer/Getty Images; Page 144b: Time & Life Pictures/Getty Images; Page 145tl: Corbis; Pages 145tr–148t: Bettmann/Corbis; Page 148bl: Ed Clark/Getty Images; Page 148br: Hulton Archive/Getty Images; Page 149t: Hulton Archive/Getty Images; Page 149b: Time & Life Pictures/Getty Images; Pages 152–154t: Bettmann/Corbis; Page 154b: The White House Historical Association; Page 155t: Bettmann/Corbis; Page 155b: Alfred Eisenstaedt/Getty Images; Page 158t: Corbis; Page 158b: Getty Images; Pages 159–160: Bettmann/Corbis; Page 161tl: The White House Historical Association; Page 161tr: Getty Images/Handout; Page 164: Bettmann/Corbis; Page 165t: Arthur Schatz/Getty Images; Page 165b: Getty Images; Page 166t: Hulton Archive/Getty Images; Page 166b: Bettmann/Corbis; Pages 169–170: George Bush Presidential Library and Museum; Page 171t: Bettmann/Corbis; Page 171b: Stefan Zaklin/epa/Corbis; Page 172: Getty Images News; Page 173: Cynthia Johnson/Getty Images; Page 177: Alfred Eisenstaedt/Getty Images; Page 178: Associated Press; Page 179t: Clinton Presidential Library; Page 179b: Downing Larry/Corbis Sygma; Page 184: Mannie Garcia/Reuters/Corbis; Page 185: Shaun Heasley/Reuters/Corbis; Page 186t: Brooks Kraft/Corbis; Page 186b: Shelly Katz/Getty Images; Page 187t: Shealah Craighead/White House/Handout/CNP/Corbis; Page 187b: Brian Snyder/Reuters/Corbis; Page 191: Brooks Kraft/Corbis; Pages 192–193t: Tim Llewellyn/Corbis; Page 193b: John Gress/Reuters/Corbis; Page 204: Kerry Beyer/Kerry Beyer Photography; Pages 206–207: Shutterstock. All clip art courtesy of clipart.com.

Noah McCullough is a proud American teenager who is taking patriotism seriously and to a new level. He is preparing himself now to lead our nation as commander in chief in 2032. Noah is passionate about United States history and believes part of his mission involves getting others "hooked on history," especially young people. He contends that if more young people knew the history of the United States, there would be no question as to whether they would vote when old enough and be involved in solutions and service to our country. Noah's fascination with U.S. presidents happened as a result of the 2000 election. As a kindergardener, he was intrigued about the electoral college, party system, campaigning, and the fact that all through history presidents have shown themselves to be ordinary people serving in an extraordinary position. Noah's thirst for knowledge and love of books sent him on a lifelong quest to know more about the great country he lives in as well as to be of service to it.

Noah has appeared on *The Tonight Show With Jay Leno* many times as a political correspondent and history whiz kid. Viewers nationwide have been impressed by his quick wit, knowledge, and quest to serve. He has also appeared on *Oprah Winfrey, Martha Stewart, The Today Show,* and many news programs. Noah was a Scholastic Kids Press reporter for the 2004 election year and at the 2005 inauguration. At the age of ten, Noah became a published author. *The Essential Book of Presidential Trivia* was published by Random House in 2006. *First Kids* is his second book.

Inspiration is what keeps Noah going. He is inspired by each and every president that has led this nation. Currently he is committed to helping raise money for research that will cure diseases as well as solving the Social Security problem. Noah keeps busy speaking all over the United States. He speaks in elementary, middle, and high schools about being altruistic and making a difference. He also speaks at churches, corporate events, political events, conventions, and motivational conferences. Noah is in pursuit of his dream to be president by living a life of excellence and service. However, he is also a regular kid who enjoys music, basketball, football, sports statistics, video games, and pizza (not necessarily in that order).

Noah's motto remains "Vote for me in 2032 on the Republican ticket!" He urges you to read his books and others about our nation's history!